GALLUP PRESS
1330 Avenue of the Americas
17th Floor
New York, NY 10019

Library of Congress Control Number: 2017957145

ISBN: 978-1-59562-208-2

First Printing: 2017
10 9 8 7 6 5 4 3 2 1

Copyright © 2017 Gallup, Inc.

"We change the world one client at a time through extraordinary analytics and advice on everything important facing humankind."

– JIM CLIFTON, CHAIRMAN AND CEO

About This Report

GALLUP'S *STATE OF THE GLOBAL WORKPLACE* report summarizes a wealth of data on how effectively employers and countries around the world are using the human capital in their workforces. Gallup World Poll results from 155 countries provide the context to discuss labor markets and workplace conditions across global regions. The report covers a series of strategies for maximizing workplace productivity, reveals regional workforce metrics and features country-specific spotlight articles that offer insights from Gallup's workplace consultants around the world.

ABOUT GALLUP

Gallup delivers analytics and advice to help leaders and organizations solve their most pressing problems. Combining more than 80 years of experience with our global reach, Gallup knows more about the attitudes and behaviors of employees, customers, students and citizens than any other organization in the world.

For more information about Gallup solutions for optimizing business performance, please visit Gallup.com/contact.

From the Chairman and CEO

GLOBAL PRODUCTIVITY GROWTH IS IN DECLINE.

GDP PER CAPITA — OR PRODUCTIVITY — is a key metric in global economics. It is the starting point for measuring almost everything having to do with economic growth and human development.

When the world's productivity is in decline, so is the availability of good jobs with a living wage. Poor productivity stunts societal and economic growth.

My conclusion from reading this report is that global productivity can be fixed. Executives and a wide variety of team leaders at many different levels could change the world's productivity quickly.

Gallup analytics find that "There is someone at work who encourages my development" is one of the best survey questions that separates enthusiastic, high-performing workers from low-performing, miserable ones.

The Fix for Declining Productivity

1. Move the whole world to a workplace strategy of "high development." The single best activity for any team leader to deliver is not employee satisfaction, but rather employee *development*.

2. Make every workplace in the world strengths-based. The current practice of management — which attempts to turn weaknesses into strengths — doesn't work. Moving to strengths-based workplaces will change global productivity and growth overnight.

3. Move the world's workplace mission from paycheck to purpose. Of course, all employees need fair pay. But they are now driven more than ever by mission and purpose and require a workplace culture that delivers it.

4. Move the whole world to one workplace metric. Use the Gallup Q^{12} as you would Net Promoter Score — but for employees. The Gallup Q^{12} has more tested and validated survey items with more analytics, breakthroughs and discoveries than any other employee measurement system in the world. These are the right benchmarks for any organization. And it serves all of us when we use the same metrics and language.

According to this report, worldwide employee engagement is only 15%. What if we doubled that? What if we tripled it? Imagine how quickly that would fix global GDP, productivity and hence, human development.

Jim Clifton
Chairman and CEO

Executive Summary

A CLOSER LOOK AT THE WORLD'S WORKFORCES

ALMOST A DECADE AFTER THE onset of the Great Recession, the world economy continues to struggle. The global gross domestic product has puttered along at under 3% growth since 2012, well below historical norms. Widespread joblessness — particularly among young people — has led to social and political strife in many areas. Since 2015, economic frustrations have likely contributed to a rise in nationalism and growing resentment toward immigrants, particularly in the U.S. and Europe.

The resulting social and political volatility is not just a government issue. These conditions dampen business development as skittish investors weigh increased risk. To achieve productivity gains while avoiding the instability that disrupts sustainable growth, governments and businesses alike need to place new focus on the resources and strategies they use to develop and empower their citizens and workforces. Broad-based strategies for human capital development give more individuals a stake in the success of their employer or their country, boosting their motivation and reducing the potential for conflict.

For governments, the goal is to expand the availability of high-quality jobs and the number of residents qualified to take them. Gallup's global surveys from 2014 to 2016 indicate that 32% of working-age adults across 155 countries are employed full time for an employer — an important measure of the availability of good jobs.

However, Gallup's workplace analytics identify immense room for productivity gains among those employees. Worldwide, the percentage of adults who work full time for an employer and are engaged at work — they are highly involved in and enthusiastic about their work and workplace — is just 15%. That low percentage of engaged employees is a barrier to creating high-performing cultures. It implies a stunning amount of wasted potential, given that business units in the top quartile of our global employee engagement database are 17% more productive and 21% more profitable than those in the bottom quartile.

Why is the global proportion of employees who are engaged in their work so low? There are many potential reasons — but resistance to change is a common underlying theme in Gallup's research and experience. In particular, organizations and institutions have often been slow to adapt to the rapid changes produced by the spread of information technology, the globalization of markets for products and labor, the rise of the gig economy, and younger workers' unique expectations. Business and political leaders must recognize when traditional patterns in management practices, education or gender roles, for example, become roadblocks to workers' motivation and productivity, and when selectively disrupting tradition will help clear a path to greater prosperity and transformed company cultures.

Improving Productivity by Working Toward a More Employee-Centered World

A few patterns in Gallup's global employee engagement data are consistent worldwide. For example, in virtually all regions, employee engagement levels tend to be lower in industries characterized by more routinized jobs, such as manufacturing and production. The conventional management mentality in these industries often puts process ahead of people, contrary to the employee-centered focus that promotes improved business performance.

However, some differences in employee engagement across global regions can't be attributed to macroeconomic factors like the prevalence of different job types. One of the most surprising differences is that the proportion of engaged employees in Western Europe — one of the world's most economically developed regions — is even lower than the global average. Only 10% of employed Western Europeans are engaged at work; by comparison, the figure among U.S. employees is more than three times as high, at 33%. The contrast suggests that management practices are a key factor in U.S. companies' ongoing productivity edge over their European counterparts.

Businesses that orient performance management systems around basic human needs for psychological engagement — such as positive workplace relationships, frequent recognition, ongoing performance conversations and opportunities for personal development — get the most out of their employees. However, Gallup global engagement analytics suggest that those conditions are less common in some cultural settings than in others. For example, a strong historical tradition of hierarchical leadership — such as in East Asia, where just 6% of employees are engaged at work — may contribute to company cultures that make it more difficult for managers to adopt a "coaching" mindset that places more emphasis on what employees need to reach their potential for productivity and other business outcomes.

In some cases, however, the capacity for increased workforce productivity may depend on an organization's ability to overcome hurdles so they can adapt to changing circumstances. In Japan, for example, businesses face an urgent need to focus on people management to counter a culture of overwork that has led to increased rates of serious physical and mental health problems. Japanese businesses also need more employee-centered management practices if they are to tap into potential productivity gains from one of the country's most undervalued resources: working women.

Building Strengths-Based Workplaces to Unleash Employees' Potential

One of the most important ways in which command-and-control leadership can stifle productivity is by denying employees the flexibility to gravitate toward roles and responsibilities that play to their inherent abilities. Strategies that allow individuals to identify, develop and use their natural talents so they become strengths have the potential to dramatically improve workforce productivity.

Employees who use their strengths on the job are more likely than others to be intrinsically motivated by their work — simply because it feels less like work to them. At the workgroup level, team members who know each other's strengths relate more effectively to one another, boosting group cohesion. In a study of almost 50,000 business units in 45 countries, Gallup researchers discovered that workgroups that received strengths interventions saw sales increase by 10% to 19% and profits by 14% to 29%, compared with control groups.

In many cases, making better use of employees' strengths will require businesses to grant workers greater input and autonomy to use those strengths. This approach often requires a profound shift in management perspective, as traditional manager-employee power dynamics give way to more personalized relationships through which managers position their team members for maximum impact according to their individual strengths.

The resulting sense of empowerment benefits both the employee and the organization. Employees who strongly agree that their opinions count at work are more likely to feel personally invested in their job. Gallup's global data suggest that without such opportunities, workers are more likely to doubt their ability to get ahead by working hard — a devastating blow to their motivation and productivity. Higher levels of autonomy also promote the development and implementation of new ideas as employees feel empowered to pursue entrepreneurial goals that benefit the organization — that is, to be "intrapreneurs."

Hiring Great Managers to Implement Positive Change

Workgroup managers are the most critical players in the effort to implement performance management systems that are performance-oriented, engagement-based and strengths-focused. Gallup's workplace analytics and experience have shown that unhappy employees often leave their job because of a poor relationship with a manager. Conversely, talented managers naturally help maximize productivity by building strong, positive relationships. They work to understand employees' sources of intrinsic motivation — the talents and goals that keep them focused and help them achieve.

That individualized approach helps great managers account for generational differences in employee expectations, such as a lack of tolerance among millennial employees — particularly in more economically developed regions — for workplaces they believe stunt their growth. On the other hand, in China and other countries that have historically emphasized respect for elders, older workers may be put off by the idea that their manager should also act as their "coach," so managers may need to adopt a more deferential approach. Great managers understand these differing perspectives and develop flexible strategies for engaging each employee accordingly.

As the broad discrepancies in workforce productivity around the world demonstrate, maximizing the value of human capital is not an easy proposition. It's a goal that requires strategic efforts at various societal levels, from national populations to businesses and organizations to individual residents. It requires leaders to understand when past behaviors and traditions will no longer lead to future prosperity and success. When employers and public officials align to establish the conditions that promote productivity, resilience and self-determination in their workforces, they are far more likely to tap the economic energy they need for sustainable growth.

Business leaders have a pivotal role to play in this process. Among the best-managed companies in Gallup's database, as many as 70% of employees are engaged, demonstrating the vast potential for improvement on this measure — one that is associated with gains in productivity and other key business outcomes. Companies that prioritize employee engagement will be the ones that help their country achieve social stability and higher living standards. And the jobs they create will provide residents not only with financial security, but also with a sense of self-worth and optimism about the future.

For more information about Gallup's research on the challenges and opportunities currently facing workplaces around the world, see our complete *State of the Global Workplace* report. The report features chapters addressing each of the major themes discussed here, as well as sections on each region and spotlight articles with input from Gallup consultants around the globe.

Businesses that orient performance management systems around basic human needs for psychological engagement get the most out of their employees.

This report covers strategies for maximizing workplace productivity, reveals regional workforce metrics and features country-specific articles that offer insights from Gallup's workplace consultants around the world.

TABLE OF CONTENTS

01

Untapped Human Capital: The Next Great Global Resource

32%

*of working–age adults worldwide
have a "good job."*

WE START WITH A BASIC question about the job market in a given country: How many residents have a good job? Gallup defines a "good job" as any full-time work for an employer. In more economically developed countries, small and medium-sized enterprises (SMEs) account for most employment. Less developed countries, by contrast, have a few large employers (typically including the government) but very few SMEs. In these countries, many residents are engaged in microenterprises. They eke out a living in subsistence activities like small-scale farming, even though this work offers little opportunity for them to progress toward a better future. It is all they have in the absence of good jobs.

In macroeconomic terms, work at subsistence level does nothing to increase per-person productivity — the factor that drives economic development. Rapidly rising productivity in some countries but not others has led to huge disparities in global living standards, particularly since the technological advances of the Industrial Revolution in the 19th century.

These gaps underlie much of the suffering and instability in the world today, and they are nowhere more clearly reflected than in the availability of good jobs around the world. It has become increasingly clear that promoting job growth, particularly in countries where it is most desperately needed, requires a coordinated effort by societal and business leaders.

- Political leaders must work to ensure that supports for human capital development are in place — most importantly, to provide equitable education opportunities that align with the country's labor market needs and promote adaptability amid rapid technological changes.

- Employers, especially those in the private sector, must ensure that they are prepared to make the most of the resulting human capital by creating workplace cultures that drive performance development and allow individuals to make the best use of their time and talents.

Leaders who work together on conditions that maximize productivity and resilience along the education-employment spectrum offer the best hope for the job growth that many countries need to escape economic stagnation. The goal is to generate sustainable economic energy with the factors that promote human capital development at three levels: societies, employers and individuals.

Though Gallup research evaluates factors at all three levels, this report primarily focuses on employers' role in the process.

INDIVIDUAL-LEVEL SUPPORTS: Supports for human capital development at the individual level include tools that promote self-awareness and strengths development and mentoring programs such as those on career development or financial health.

PERSONAL DEVELOPMENT AND FOCUS ON STRENGTHS: Unlocking human potential through personal development and a focus on individuals' innate strengths requires commitment by both employers and individuals.

EMPLOYER-LEVEL SUPPORTS: *State of the Global Workplace* describes employers' roles in developing human capital to maximize their productivity and drive growth. Most of the world's businesses and organizations fall short in establishing these supports, resulting in wasted potential.

EDUCATION-WORKFORCE TIES AND ENTREPRENEURSHIP TRAINING AND FINANCING: Some supports require coordinated efforts at the societal and organizational levels. Examples include support for new business startups and education-workforce ties such as internships.

SOCIETY-LEVEL SUPPORTS: Society-level supports are mostly in the public policy domain; responsible governments lay the foundation for human capital development by guaranteeing security and rule of law and ensuring equitable access to essential services like education and healthcare. Public-private partnerships often expand access to these and other vital supports, such as financial and IT services.

HUMAN CAPITAL DEVELOPMENT MODEL

Human capital development requires strategies for empowering people at various levels of society, from national institutions to public or private employers to individuals.

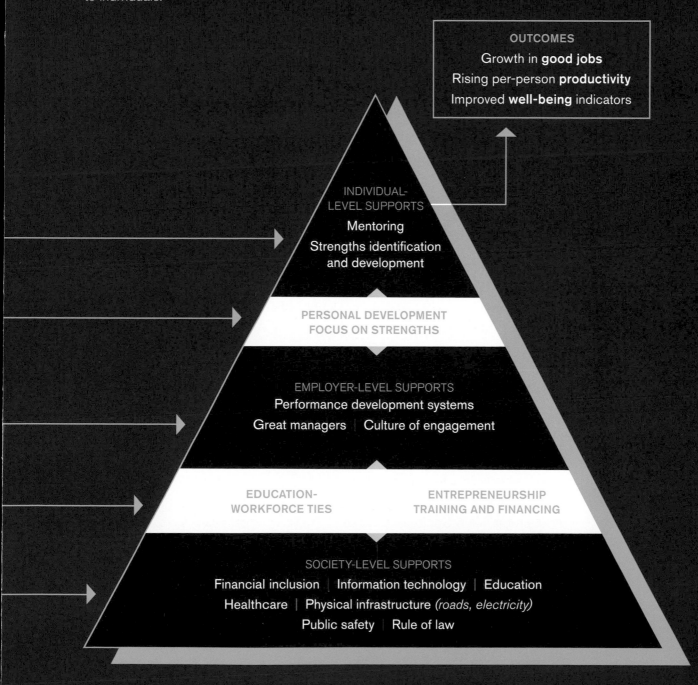

OUTCOMES
Growth in **good jobs**
Rising per-person **productivity**
Improved **well-being** indicators

INDIVIDUAL-LEVEL SUPPORTS
Mentoring
Strengths identification and development

PERSONAL DEVELOPMENT FOCUS ON STRENGTHS

EMPLOYER-LEVEL SUPPORTS
Performance development systems
Great managers | Culture of engagement

EDUCATION-WORKFORCE TIES

ENTREPRENEURSHIP TRAINING AND FINANCING

SOCIETY-LEVEL SUPPORTS
Financial inclusion | Information technology | Education
Healthcare | Physical infrastructure *(roads, electricity)*
Public safety | Rule of law

GOOD JOBS RATE VARIES WIDELY THROUGHOUT WORLD

Close to one-third of working-age adults around the world work full time (at least 30 hours per week) for an employer — our definition of a good job. More specifically, 32% of residents aged 23 to 65[1] across the 155 countries surveyed for Gallup World Polls conducted from 2014 to 2016 fall into this category.

At the country level, the good jobs rate ranges from 5% in Niger to 72% in the United Arab Emirates. In the world's poorest region, sub-Saharan Africa, the good jobs rate exceeds 30% only in the tiny island nation of Mauritius (42%); by contrast, in Western Europe, it falls below 40% only in Italy (36%), Spain (37%) and Ireland (39%).

These good jobs data can be segmented in countless ways to produce insights on how local conditions influence employment opportunities. A broad look at results by global region gives a bird's-eye view of how the availability of full-time work for employers varies by economic development level. For example, working-age residents in the U.S./Canada are about four times more likely than residents in sub-Saharan Africa to hold a good job (56% vs. 14%, respectively).

Comparing the results for men and women offers a look at how traditional gender roles may affect levels of full-time employment. Gender gaps in the percentage of residents who are employed full time for an employer are largest in the Middle East/North Africa region and South Asia; these regions have among the lowest proportions of residents working full time for an employer, largely because of the unusually low percentages of women with a good job.

1 in 3
working-age adults worldwide have a "good job."

---

1   Analysis of employment data includes respondents aged 23 to 65 with the assumption that individuals younger and older than this range are more likely to be out of the workforce for socially desirable reasons (e.g., education or retirement).

PERCENTAGE OF POPULATION EMPLOYED FULL TIME FOR AN EMPLOYER
Based on data aggregated from 2014-2016 Gallup World Polls*

	Total %	Men %	Women %	Gender gap (pct. pts.)
World (155 countries surveyed)	**32**	**42**	**23**	**19**
South Asia	28	43	14	29
Middle East/ North Africa	24	37	10	27
Latin America	32	43	22	21
Australia/ New Zealand	46	56	38	18
Southeast Asia	25	35	17	18
U.S./Canada	56	64	48	16
Post-Soviet Eurasia	50	58	44	14
East Asia	34	40	27	13
Eastern Europe	49	55	43	12
Western Europe	45	51	39	12
Sub-Saharan Africa	14	19	9	10

*Within each region, results are weighted proportionally by population size in each country. Population includes ages 23 to 65.

WHERE THE JOBS ARE
Adults aged 23-65 and employed full time for an employer
Gallup World Poll, 2014-2016

% Employed full time for
an employer

| 5% | 72% |
| Niger | UAE |

Gray countries were not included in this study. See
the appendix for "good jobs" data, by country.

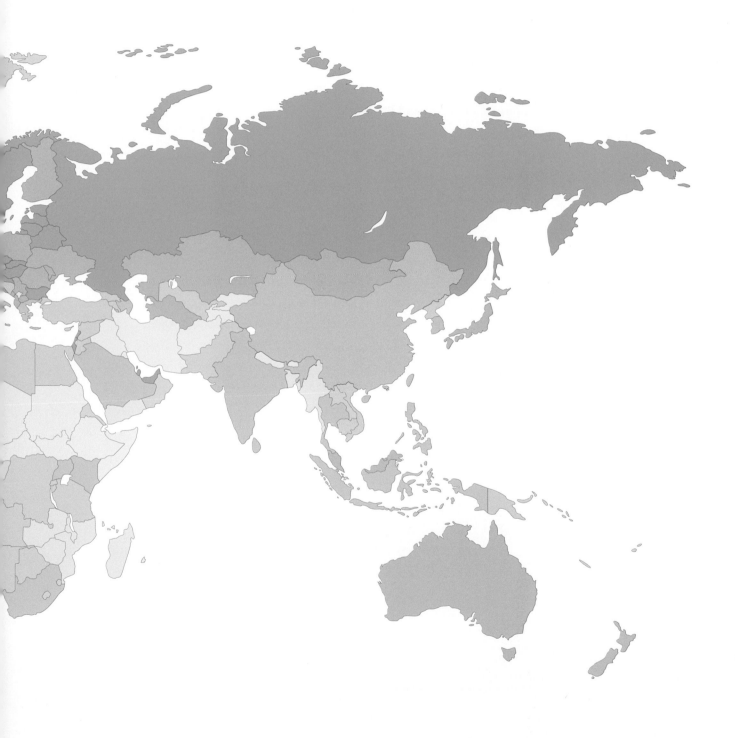

EMPLOYEE ENGAGEMENT

The global aggregate from Gallup data collected in 2014, 2015 and 2016 across 155 countries indicates that just 15% of employees worldwide are engaged in their job. Two-thirds are not engaged, and 18% are actively disengaged. The two Western-hemisphere regions — U.S./Canada and Latin America — lead the world in the percentage of employees who are engaged at work. However, at 31% and 27%, respectively, plenty of opportunity remains in each region to increase productivity through higher engagement levels.[2]

15%
of employees worldwide are engaged in their job.

In each country, residents who indicate they are employed by an employer are asked a series of questions from Gallup's $Q^{12®}$, which measures employee engagement and its impact on business outcomes. (See Chapter 2 for more information on Gallup's approach to measuring employee engagement.) The results place employees into one of three groups that characterize the extent to which they are motivated by a sense of support and emotional attachment to their employer.

- Engaged: Employees are highly involved in and enthusiastic about their work and workplace. They are psychological "owners," drive performance and innovation, and move the organization forward.

- Not engaged: Employees are psychologically unattached to their work and company. Because their engagement needs are not being fully met, they're putting time — but not energy or passion — into their work.

---

2   Notably, Gallup's World Poll surveys have consistently supported the notion that Latin Americans have a tendency to evaluate various aspects of their lives more positively on average than do respondents in other regions. This effect likely inflates employee engagement results from the region relative to those from elsewhere in the world.

- **Actively disengaged:** Employees aren't just unhappy at work — they are resentful that their needs aren't being met and are acting out their unhappiness. Every day, these workers potentially undermine what their engaged coworkers accomplish.

When analyzing the data, some of the most startling regional findings come from Western Europe. Given that it is among the world's most economically developed regions, one might expect its results — like those from the U.S./ Canada — to be among the most positive. However, just 10% of Western European employees are engaged at work, while the vast majority (71%) are not engaged, and 19% are actively disengaged. The Western Europe regional chapter offers a country-by-country breakdown of these results, as well as country spotlight articles that explore reasons for disaffection among many European workers.

Some of the most startling regional findings come from Western Europe.

10%
of employees are engaged at work.

71%
of employees are not engaged at work.

19%
of employees are actively disengaged at work.

EMPLOYEE ENGAGEMENT RESULTS AMONG RESIDENTS WHO ARE EMPLOYED FOR AN EMPLOYER

Based on data aggregated from 2014-2016 Gallup World Polls*

■ % Engaged   ■ % Not engaged   ■ % Actively disengaged

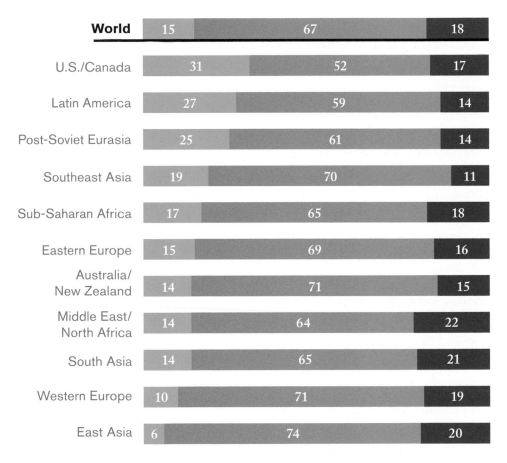

	% Engaged	% Not engaged	% Actively disengaged
World	15	67	18
U.S./Canada	31	52	17
Latin America	27	59	14
Post-Soviet Eurasia	25	61	14
Southeast Asia	19	70	11
Sub-Saharan Africa	17	65	18
Eastern Europe	15	69	16
Australia/New Zealand	14	71	15
Middle East/North Africa	14	64	22
South Asia	14	65	21
Western Europe	10	71	19
East Asia	6	74	20

*Within each region, results are weighted proportionally by population size in each country.

Engagement Levels Vary by Job Type

Gallup consistently finds that engagement levels worldwide vary by job type. Employees in knowledge-based jobs, such as managers and professionals in various fields, are more likely to be engaged in their work than are those in more routinized roles, such as clerical or manufacturing jobs. For example, among professional workers worldwide, those who are engaged outnumber those who are actively disengaged by more than two to one, while among manufacturing and construction workers, twice as many employees are actively disengaged as are engaged.

This makes sense given the kinds of workplace conditions that strengthen engagement: opportunities for workers to voice their opinions, to expand their skill sets and to use their unique combination of strengths. Gallup has consistently found that manufacturing workers, in particular, struggle with engagement. The conventional management mentality in this industry tends to put process ahead of people, which runs counter to the employee-centered focus that promotes engagement.

More generally, traditional command-and-control management models remain common throughout the world. Employees in production or service roles, for example, may have little say in determining how their day is structured or what could be done to improve their job or workplace. Comparatively, employees in professional or managerial roles may find it easier to set their own priorities and to share their opinions, helping to boost their engagement.

> *Employees in knowledge-based jobs, such as managers and professionals in various fields, are more likely to be engaged in their work than are those in more routinized roles, such as clerical or manufacturing jobs.*

ENGAGEMENT AMONG EMPLOYED RESIDENTS WORLDWIDE

	Engaged %	Not engaged %	Actively disengaged %
Manager/Executive/Official: in a business or the government	28	63	9
Professional: doctor, lawyer, engineer, teacher, nurse, etc.	27	62	11
Service worker: maid, taxi driver, maintenance or repair worker, etc.	18	64	18
Farmer/Fisherman/Other agricultural laborer	18	60	22
Clerical/Other office worker/ Sales worker	14	72	14
Construction/Manufacturing/ Production worker	12	64	24

The good news is that, in the long run, the shift to more knowledge-based work that results from technological advances and economic development generally means more people have opportunities to be engaged at work. In knowledge-based economies with equitable educational opportunities, many workers will be able to focus their education on areas of natural strength and move into jobs where they — and their employers — can reap the benefits of improved employee engagement.

The bad news is that such development often does not happen very equitably. Many employees in manual or highly routinized jobs are let go and have little opportunity to acquire the skills and knowledge needed for a new job in the growing knowledge-based sectors. And those who do retain their job may feel more dismal about their own working conditions amid the spread of knowledge-based industries.

For example, manufacturing companies that fail to consider workers' individual goals and needs stand in sharp contrast to U.S. information technology companies, many of which are known for going to great lengths to support and retain their employees. Considering individual goals and needs is a critical management challenge for employers in manufacturing, retail and other sectors that, in many cases, don't require advanced education or skill levels.

However, it's a challenge that many organizations meet by focusing on the same essential elements of engagement that motivate workers in other roles. Managers in more routinized sectors often place particular focus on elements that heighten employees' sense of accomplishment, such as frequent recognition and opportunities for personal development.

"BRAIN DRAIN," EMIGRATION OF HIGHLY EDUCATED WORKERS

One of the most critical questions for many leaders who are focused on developing their country's stock of human capital is how to retain employees in high-skill positions. The desire among highly educated workers to emigrate in search of better job opportunities is particularly common in several developing regions — places where highly educated individuals are most desperately needed, including in sub-Saharan Africa, Latin America and the Middle East/North Africa region.

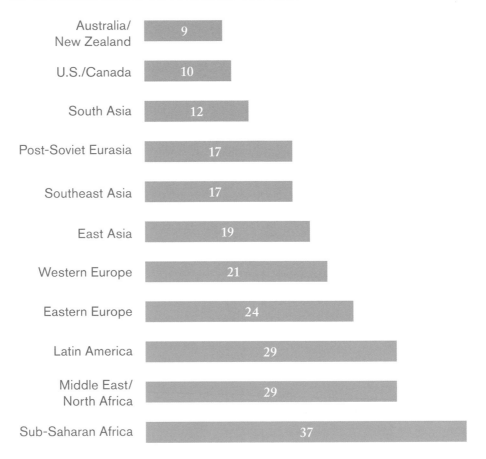

PERCENTAGE OF HIGHLY EDUCATED EMPLOYEES WHO WOULD LIKE TO MOVE PERMANENTLY TO ANOTHER COUNTRY

Region	Percentage
Australia/New Zealand	9
U.S./Canada	10
South Asia	12
Post-Soviet Eurasia	17
Southeast Asia	17
East Asia	19
Western Europe	21
Eastern Europe	24
Latin America	29
Middle East/North Africa	29
Sub-Saharan Africa	37

Workplace cultures that promote engagement may be an important part of the solution. In almost all regions, the desire to emigrate among highly educated employees varies significantly by engagement level. Specifically, actively disengaged employees are most likely to want to move permanently to another country — often by a substantial margin. For example, in Western Europe, 40% of actively disengaged employees respond this way versus 16% of engaged employees.

These results suggest that one way to reduce the "brain drain" problem in many countries is to focus on moving highly skilled workers out of the actively disengaged column. Often, actively disengaged employees have a specific reason for harboring feelings of resentment toward their employer.

They may feel stuck with a manager who doesn't understand or care about them, for example, or that their employer is failing to fulfill basic conditions promised to employees when they were hired — conditions that were part of their formal contract or were less formal but clearly implied.

Whatever the reason, employers seeking to retain actively disengaged employees must first understand the source of their discontent and then make every effort to remove barriers to engagement. Examining the way such employees are managed is a good place to start. One Gallup study in Germany found that unemployed Germans were less likely to experience negative emotions like sadness, stress and anger than were those who worked for bad managers.

PRODUCTIVITY GAINS REQUIRE UNDERSTANDING WHAT MAKES EMPLOYEES "TICK"

Raising the productivity and creativity of workforces is a goal that will have to be addressed on multiple fronts. At the societal level, many countries have work to do in bolstering the rule of law and improving critical supports for human capital development, including education and healthcare, to lay the groundwork for rising productivity. At the workplace level, employers need new strategies for ensuring that workers' day-to-day experiences keep them motivated and make the most of their abilities. These areas are interrelated, and each requires careful tracking and input, particularly from the perspective of workers.

But the potential benefit to putting in this effort is immense. In much the same way that developing countries have bypassed the need for expensive landline telecom infrastructure by promoting wireless networks, businesses in emerging markets have opportunities to evade outdated — and often costly — approaches to performance management and employee engagement. They must start by recognizing that an organization's

Employers need new strategies for ensuring that workers' day-to-day experiences keep them motivated and make the most of their abilities.

vitality and capacity for organic growth is inextricably tied to the everyday experiences of its employees.

Effective approaches to maximizing human capital within organizations include:

1. using management tools that track and improve the essential workplace conditions that keep employees engaged and motivated

2. having a focus on identifying and leveraging the strengths of every employee

3. developing an understanding of how to cultivate innovation and entrepreneurial talent to promote new sources of growth from within the organization

Gallup has developed these approaches over decades of workplace research, and they are proven to be highly effective across a wide range of industries and organizational types.

The return on investment in any one of these strategies is potentially great — but the strategies also are complementary and can have a transformative effect on workplace productivity when used in tandem. Just as importantly, they can shift the mindset of an organization's leadership to one that puts human capital development first and, consequently, gain a far more reliable foundation for future prosperity.

Businesses must recognize that an organization's vitality and capacity for organic growth is inextricably tied to the everyday experiences of its employees.

02

High-Performing Workplace Cultures Need Engaged Employees

33

85%

of adults worldwide
are not engaged or are
actively disengaged.

TODAY'S WORKPLACES AND LEADERS ARE facing mounting pressures due to new types of work arrangements, challenges to traditional management styles and shifting expectations from workers. In response, most leaders who Gallup works with understand the importance of creating high-performing cultures; however, not all leaders understand or maximize the potential of current employees to create this competitive advantage.

Gallup's surveys with employees around the world find that just 15% are currently engaged at work — that is, psychologically invested in their job and motivated to be highly productive. Two-thirds worldwide (67%) are not engaged, putting in time but little discretionary effort at work, and 18% are actively disengaged — openly resentful that their workplace needs aren't being met.

However, these employee data vary significantly by industry and region, raising the question: Is workplace engagement a concept that "travels" well? In other words, is it relevant across cultural and economic contexts, as well as different job types?

Generally, the answer is yes because Gallup's Q^{12} engagement metric addresses only the most fundamental aspects of human nature as it relates to employment, such as the need for positive relationships, developmental opportunities and a sense of purpose. While strategies for improving these conditions must be tailored to specific workplace environments, the conditions themselves are associated with positive business outcomes across a broad range of industries and locations.

Gallup's work with organizations around the world demonstrates that the variation in employee engagement among *employers* within countries can be far greater than the variation among *countries*. Across regional and cultural contexts, there are companies that buck national engagement trends, outperforming their domestic and international competitors and creating workplace cultures that focus on meeting employees' needs to drive high performance.

These exceptional companies recognize that engaged employees are the fuel of the organization, and they own this from the top of the house to the front lines. They include many past winners of the Gallup Great Workplace Award (GGWA). The award honors a select group of organizations that focus on systematically creating a highly engaged and high-performing workplace. GGWA winners boast a remarkable ratio of 14 engaged employees for every one actively disengaged employee. Among award recipients from the past three years are organizations operating in various cultural and business environments:

- China Merchants Property Development: real estate services organization headquartered in Shenzhen, China

- NXP Semiconductors: global semiconductor manufacturer headquartered in Eindhoven, Netherlands

- Indian Hotels Company Ltd.: chain of hotels and resorts headquartered in Mumbai, India

- NFU Mutual: insurance, investment and financial services organization headquartered in Stratford-upon-Avon, U.K.

- Mashreq Bank: banking services organization headquartered in Dubai, United Arab Emirates

HIGHER EMPLOYEE ENGAGEMENT LEVELS ARE LINKED TO A RANGE OF POSITIVE BUSINESS OUTCOMES

All of the companies listed on the previous page have experienced healthy growth and other successes in recent years, largely as a result of the performance of their workforce. In 2016, Gallup conducted the ninth version of our meta-analysis (study of studies) to determine the relationship between engagement — as measured by the Q^{12} — and business/work unit profitability, productivity, employee retention and customer perceptions. Despite massive changes in the economy and technology, the results of the most recent meta-analysis are consistent with the results of previous versions. Simply put, engaged employees produce better business outcomes than do other employees across industry, across company size and nationality, and in good economic times and bad.

Business or work units that score in the top quartile of their organization in employee engagement have nearly double the odds of success (based on a composite of financial, customer, retention, safety, quality, shrinkage and absenteeism metrics) when compared with those in the bottom quartile. Those at the 99th percentile have four times the success rate of those at the first percentile.

WHEN COMPARED WITH BUSINESS UNITS IN THE BOTTOM
QUARTILE OF ENGAGEMENT, THOSE IN THE TOP QUARTILE
REALIZE IMPROVEMENTS IN THE FOLLOWING AREAS:

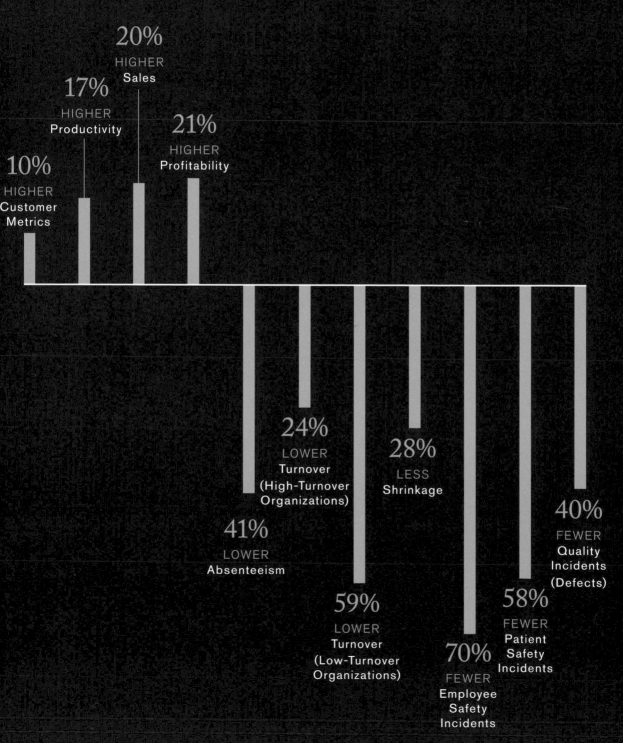

20%
HIGHER
Sales

17%
HIGHER
Productivity

21%
HIGHER
Profitability

10%
HIGHER
Customer
Metrics

24%
LOWER
Turnover
(High-Turnover
Organizations)

28%
LESS
Shrinkage

41%
LOWER
Absenteeism

40%
FEWER
Quality
Incidents
(Defects)

59%
LOWER
Turnover
(Low-Turnover
Organizations)

58%
FEWER
Patient
Safety
Incidents

70%
FEWER
Employee
Safety
Incidents

Showing up and staying. Engaged employees make it a point to show up to work and do more work — highly engaged business units realize 41% lower absenteeism and 17% higher productivity. Engaged workers also are more likely to stay with their employer. In organizations with high employee turnover, highly engaged business units achieve 24% lower turnover. In those with low employee turnover, the gains are even more dramatic: Highly engaged business units achieve 59% lower turnover. High-turnover organizations are those with more than 40% annualized turnover, and low-turnover organizations are those with 40% or lower annualized turnover.

Shrinkage and quality. Engaged workers care more about the products and services they deliver to customers and the overall performance of their organization. Highly engaged business units experience 28% less shrinkage (the dollar amount of unaccounted-for merchandise) and 40% fewer quality incidents (defects).

Safety. Engaged workers are more mindful of their surroundings. They are aware of safety procedures and are diligent about keeping their coworkers and customers protected. Highly engaged business units realize 70% fewer safety incidents and 58% fewer patient safety incidents.

Customer outcomes. Employees who are engaged consistently show up to work and have a greater commitment to quality and safety. Understandably, these employees also help their organization improve customer relationships and obtain impressive organic growth. Highly engaged business units achieve 10% higher customer metrics and 20% higher sales.

Profit. The aforementioned outcomes converge to bring organizations increased profitability. Engaged employees are more present and productive; they are more attuned to the needs of customers; and they are more observant of processes, standards and systems. The behaviors of highly engaged business units result in 21% higher profitability.

Gallup's research also shows that companies with engaged workforces have higher earnings per share (EPS). In a recent study, we examined publicly traded companies with EPS data available from 2011 to 2015 and found that winners of the Gallup Great Workplace Award outperformed their competitors who did not win. This finding is consistent with previous analyses of the relationship between engagement and EPS.

Specifically, when comparing EPS from 2011 to 2013 with 2014 to 2015:

- Publicly traded organizations that received the Gallup Great Workplace Award experienced 115% growth in EPS, while their competitors experienced 27% growth over the same time period.

- The EPS of the best-practice organizations grew at a rate that was 4.3 times greater than that of their competitors.

- The best-practice organizations in the study had 11 engaged employees for every one actively disengaged employee. At the beginning of their engagement journey with Gallup, these organizations had an average of two engaged employees for every one actively disengaged employee.

EMPLOYEE ENGAGEMENT: A PRIMER

Gallup measures employee engagement using a 12-element survey (Gallup's Q^{12}) rooted in employees' performance management needs. When those needs are met, employees become emotionally and psychologically attached to their work and workplace. As a result, their individual performance soars, and they propel their team and organization to improved crucial outcomes such as higher levels of productivity, safety and quality.

Specifically, the Q^{12} is based on four types — or levels — of employees' performance development needs:

1. basic needs

2. individual needs

3. teamwork needs

4. personal growth needs

GALLUP'S Q¹²

■ BASIC NEEDS ■ INDIVIDUAL NEEDS ■ TEAMWORK NEEDS ■ GROWTH NEEDS

Q01: I know what is expected of me at work.

Q02: I have the materials and equipment I need to do my work right.

Q03: At work, I have the opportunity to do what I do best every day.

Q04: In the last seven days, I have received recognition or praise for doing good work.

Q05: My supervisor, or someone at work, seems to care about me as a person.

Q06: There is someone at work who encourages my development.

Q07: At work, my opinions seem to count.

Q08: The mission or purpose of my company makes me feel my job is important.

Q09: My associates or fellow employees are committed to doing quality work.

Q10: I have a best friend at work.

Q11: In the last six months, someone at work has talked to me about my progress.

Q12: This last year, I have had opportunities at work to learn and grow.

Engaged: Employees are highly involved in and enthusiastic about their work and workplace. They are psychological "owners," drive performance and innovation, and move the organization forward.

Not engaged: Employees are psychologically unattached to their work and company. Because their engagement needs are not being fully met, they're putting time — but not energy or passion — into their work.

Actively disengaged: Employees aren't just unhappy at work — they are resentful that their needs aren't being met and are acting out their unhappiness. Every day, these workers potentially undermine what their engaged coworkers accomplish.

Employees need to be equipped to perform and then positioned for individual and team success. The first, second and third levels create an environment of trust and support that enables managers and employees to get the most out of the fourth level.

These levels provide a road map for managers to motivate and develop their team members and improve the team members' performance, with each level building on the previous.

Employees need to be equipped to perform and then positioned for individual and team success.

For example, employees may feel connected to their team members, but if, among other challenges, they don't know what's expected of them (a basic need), don't have the appropriate materials and equipment (a basic need) or are not able to do what they do best (an individual need), their affiliation with their team members is unlikely to have a positive impact on their performance. Instead, time spent with their peers may more closely resemble a gripe session than productive teamwork.

The levels do not represent phases. Managers do not "finish" the first level and then move on to the second level. They must ensure that employees know what is expected of them and have the right materials and equipment to do their work while meeting needs on the second, third and fourth levels. The best way to sustain progress is to keep doing more of what works and using this hierarchy as a framework for understanding how to best support employees, determine barriers to success and adjust accordingly. Managers should, with their team members, identify needs and obstacles on an ongoing basis and ideally take action before challenges inhibit employees' performance.

REAL GROWTH REQUIRES MORE THAN A SURVEY

For many leaders and managers, creating a culture of high performance is a steadfast goal but one that remains elusive because too many organizations focus primarily on measuring engagement rather than on taking the actions needed to engage employees. Gallup has repeatedly found that one of the greatest barriers to engaging employees is a misguided notion of what employee engagement actually is and what it is meant to do. Many well-intentioned organizations make a common mistake: They make higher engagement results themselves the goal rather than focusing on the *improved performance outcomes* that higher engagement should help them achieve.

Employee engagement measures that have become increasingly commoditized and transactional in nature can promote this ineffective focus. These products help organizations gather information, but many fail to provide the necessary insights on using the data to create cultural change. Too often, the results of using such products are shallow or short-term tactics that may move the needle for the next round of engagement surveys but do little to improve organizational health and productivity over the long term.

THE SURVEY TRAP

When organizations put too much emphasis on measuring engagement rather than improving engagement, they fall into the "survey trap." This trap includes:

- viewing engagement as "just" a survey or program

- defining engagement as a percentage of employees who are not dissatisfied or are merely content with their employer

- relying on measures that tell leaders and managers what they want to hear

- measuring workers' satisfaction or happiness levels and providing frivolous perks

The action plans that result from measuring employee engagement shouldn't focus solely on making employees happier — they should be part of a broader strategic framework that clearly articulates how higher engagement levels result in improved business outcomes.

Make no mistake: Measurement does matter. But companies that base their engagement strategy on a survey or metrics-only solution can get caught up in a "rinse and repeat" pattern that does nothing to improve their business. They focus on engagement periodically — usually around survey time. As a result, these organizations are not able to achieve the high-performing culture they seek and tend to make false promises to employees, pledging change through intensive communication campaigns but providing little actual follow-through and leadership support.

Creating a culture of engagement requires more than completing an annual employee survey and then leaving managers on their own, hoping they will learn something from the survey results that will change the way they manage. It requires an organization to take a close look at how critical engagement elements align with their performance development and human capital strategies.

EMPLOYEES' LIKELIHOOD TO BE ACTIVELY DISENGAGED HAS FALLEN SINCE THE GREAT RECESSION

In 2016, results from Gallup's annual World Poll and Gallup Daily tracking surveys in the U.S. indicated that 17% of employees worldwide were engaged — involved in, enthusiastic about and committed to their work and workplace. That figure represents very gradual year-over-year improvement, inching up five percentage points from 2009 to 2016.

There is more encouraging news at the other end of the employee engagement spectrum: The world has seen an important decline in the number of actively disengaged employees — those who spread negativity in the workplace and often damage their organization's bottom line. They monopolize managers' time, have more on-the-job accidents, account for more quality defects, contribute to theft, miss more workdays and quit at a higher rate than engaged employees do.

Globally, the percentage of actively disengaged employees has decreased significantly since 2009.

26%   vs.   17%

2009   2016

In 2009, Gallup found that 26% of employees were actively disengaged — more than twice the proportion of engaged employees. These results seem logical when considering the jobs that were lost during the Great Recession in 2008 and 2009 — and the new responsibilities employees acquired at work to compensate for those who were let go. The global proportion of actively disengaged employees dropped eight percentage points as economic conditions improved between 2009 and 2014. In 2016, Gallup's estimate of actively disengaged employees was 17%, the same as the proportion who were engaged that year.

The world has seen an important decline in the number of actively disengaged employees — those who spread negativity in the workplace and often damage their organization's bottom line.

Regionally, the most dramatic declines in the proportion of actively disengaged employees between 2009 and 2016 occurred in Eastern Europe (30% to 14%) and post-Soviet Eurasia (37% to 12%), two regions among the hardest hit when foreign direct investment dried up in the wake of the global recession. The percentage of actively disengaged employees also fell considerably in South Asia — from 34% in 2009 to 17% in 2016. In South Asia and post-Soviet Eurasia, the engagement level that improved most substantially was employees' likelihood to agree that there is someone at work who encourages their development.

WORLDWIDE, MOST WORKERS ARE INDIFFERENT

Regional and country-level results in this report are based on World Poll data aggregated from 2014 to 2016 to ensure the samples of employees are large enough for reliable analysis. The results reveal wide variation among percentages of engaged employees in regions around the world: Employees in the U.S./Canada and Latin America demonstrate the highest levels of engagement at 31% and 27%, respectively. However, just 6% of employees in East Asia are engaged, as are 10% of employees in Western Europe.

Employees in the U.S./Canada and Latin America demonstrate the highest levels of engagement.

31%
U.S./Canada

27%
Latin America

Regardless of its place in the global rankings, every region that Gallup tracks is defined by one overarching finding: The majority of its workforce falls into the "not engaged" category. Overall, 67% of worldwide employees fall into this category, with regional averages ranging from 52% to 74%.

Leaders and managers often have a difficult time spotting employees who are not engaged. These workers are not hostile or disruptive. They do not hate their job or set out to wreak havoc. They are indifferent and will put the time — but not the energy or passion — into their role. With a majority of employees not engaged in their work, companies find it exceedingly difficult to accelerate innovation, creativity, productivity and other essential elements that go into improving organizational performance.

Employees who are not engaged represent a risk. These workers can tilt either way — good or bad. Many employees *want* a reason to be inspired. They are the "show me" group that needs an extra push to perform at their best. Imagine the effect on performance when leaders and managers push these employees in the right direction.

CREATING A HIGH-PERFORMING CULTURE

Engaging employees takes work and commitment, but it is not impossible. Exceptional workplaces share common philosophies and practices that can be applied at all organizations. Here are a few characteristics that Gallup finds in organizations that maintain high levels of engaged employees:

- **They know that engagement starts at the top.** Highly engaged organizations have highly committed leaders. These leaders understand that business outcomes are easier to achieve with an engaged workforce. As such, they are aligned in prioritizing employee performance needs as a competitive, strategic point of differentiation. They communicate openly and consistently, and they actively work on identifying and removing systemic barriers that prevent managers and employees from doing great work. They place the utmost importance on using the right metrics and hiring and developing great managers. Leaders of great workplaces also model the kind of psychological ownership that characterizes high engagement, visibly working to improve their own performance day by day.

- **They know local managers are in key positions to support employees' engagement and productivity levels.** Exemplary companies know that the experiences that inspire and encourage employees are local — they take place at the workgroup level. Gallup research shows that about 70% of the variance in engagement among workgroups can be attributed to their manager. Great companies support local managers by providing ongoing education that helps them sharpen their managerial talents and stay attuned to the factors that help promote high engagement on their team. In light of consistent evidence highlighting workgroup managers' importance, Gallup has developed a broad portfolio of development and coaching modules in several languages for employees in these critical roles.

- **They hold managers accountable for outcomes.** Great companies hold local managers accountable, not just for their team's engagement level, but also for how it relates to the team's overall performance. In some cases, that accountability is supported by network-based tools and applications that help managers track engagement-related metrics and develop individualized plans for keeping team members motivated and productive.

- **They ensure that basic engagement requirements are met before expecting an inspiring mission to matter.** Only when employees know what is expected of them, have what they need to do their job right, are a good fit for their role and feel their manager has their back will they feel invested enough to connect with proclamations of mission or values — no matter how inspiring these might sound in the head office.

- **They have a straightforward and decisive approach to performance management.** Companies with the highest engagement levels use recognition as a powerful incentive currency for developing employees' capabilities. Conversely, they see mediocrity as a hindrance to performance. These companies also know that, to drive continual performance development, managers and employees need frequent coaching conversations that help employees stay focused and energized for the future.

- **They do not pursue engagement for its own sake.** Highly engaged organizations stay focused on the *outcomes* associated with higher engagement levels, avoiding the survey trap described earlier. Whether their focus is on increasing productivity overall or on meeting organization-specific goals like lower turnover or fewer safety incidents, they have a thorough understanding of how outcomes relate to employee engagement, and they tailor engagement-based strategies accordingly.

These organizations have well-defined and comprehensive development programs for leaders and managers, and they focus on the development of individuals and teams. Employee engagement is a fundamental consideration in their strategy for making the most of their most valuable resources — the talents and energy in their workforce.

Creating a culture of engagement requires an organization to take a close look at how critical engagement elements align with their performance development and human capital strategies.

03

Strengths-Based Team Leadership

32%

of employees worldwide strongly agree they like what they do each day.

WHY IS IT SO IMPORTANT to optimize workplace conditions to support employees' productivity?

Consider the massive amount that businesses spend on labor: Payroll costs typically represent 15% to 30% of gross revenue, but in some industries, proportions of 50% or more are not uncommon. In that light, the idea that 85% of the world's employees are not engaged or are actively disengaged at work and therefore are not as motivated or productive as they could be is particularly alarming. Any asset that is operating at just 15% of capacity — but particularly one that represents such a substantial proportion of any business' operating costs — warrants attention.

If there is one area of focus with the potential to transform entire organizational cultures to better optimize their human capital, it is a strengths-based approach to management.

Gallup's late chairman Don Clifton pioneered the study of strengths in the workplace, affirming time and again over decades of research the gains associated with helping people do what they are inherently good at. As he demonstrated, employees who use their strengths on the job are more likely than others to be intrinsically motivated by their work, simply because it feels less like work to them.

> *"Your weaknesses will never develop, while your strengths will develop infinitely."*
> *— Don Clifton*

A MORE CONSTRUCTIVE BASIS FOR PERFORMANCE MANAGEMENT

Because the activities and demands of their job are more intrinsically rewarding, employees who say they use their strengths every day are 8% more productive and 15% less likely to quit their job. Moreover, managers in strengths-based organizations waste little time trying to wring adequate performance out of employees who are unsure if what they can contribute is making a difference.

In fact, adopting a strengths-based culture transforms the very nature of management, mitigating the adversity often inherent in employee-manager relationships by casting managers as developmental coaches. It requires managers who are curious about what makes people tick and who derive genuine satisfaction from helping employees hone their strengths.

Such managers intuitively recognize when an employee's strengths are ignored, overplayed or misunderstood. In their hands, performance evaluations are no longer dreaded, criticism-laced interactions that often leave employees feeling defensive and resentful. They understand that feedback and developmental coaching that focus on strengths and accomplishments tend to improve performance more effectively than do actions focused on fixing weaknesses.

Reorienting an organization around strengths is not necessarily an easy proposition; it can be a radical shift, particularly in light of conventional management theories that tend to focus on fixing employees' weaknesses. But once organizations implement strengths-based management practices, the payoff in terms of employees' motivation and productivity can be huge: Employees who use their strengths every day are six times as likely to be engaged at work as those who do not.

STRENGTHS-BASED DEVELOPMENT ENHANCES BUSINESS OUTCOMES

When companies support and develop strengths, employees are more engaged, have better performance outcomes and are less likely to leave. In a study by Gallup of ...

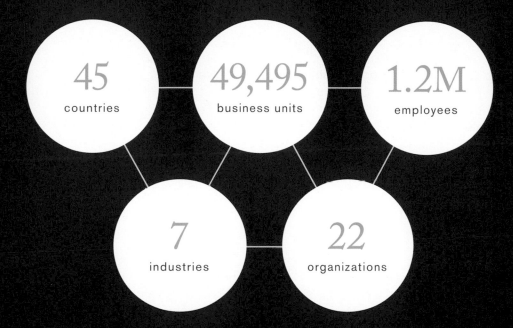

45
countries

49,495
business units

1.2M
employees

7
industries

22
organizations

... Gallup researchers discovered that, on average, workgroups that received strengths interventions saw significant improvement in sales and profits, among other measures, compared with control groups receiving less-intensive interventions or none at all.

10% TO 19%
increased sales

14% TO 29%
increased profits

STRENGTHS-BASED CULTURES ARE REWARDING FOR EMPLOYEES

Around the world, employees who strongly agree that they are able to do what they do best every day at work are far more likely than those who do not feel this way to strongly agree that:

1. they like what they do each day

2. they learn or do something interesting every day

CORRELATION BETWEEN EMPLOYEES USING THEIR STRENGTHS AND LIKING WHAT THEY DO EACH DAY

Based on data aggregated from 2014-2016 Gallup World Polls

Employees who strongly agree they like what they do each day

	Overall %	Among those who strongly agree they have an opportunity to do what they do best every day at work %
World	**32**	**60**
U.S./Canada	51	72
Latin America	52	71
South Asia	30	61
Southeast Asia	35	61
Sub-Saharan Africa	35	56
Post-Soviet Eurasia	32	53
Western Europe	29	50
Eastern Europe	25	48
East Asia	17	45
Australia/ New Zealand	21	43
Middle East/ North Africa	25	38

CORRELATION BETWEEN EMPLOYEES USING THEIR STRENGTHS AND
LEARNING EACH DAY

Based on data aggregated from 2014-2016 Gallup World Polls

| | **Employees who strongly agree they learn or do something interesting each day** | |
	Overall %	Among those who strongly agree they have an opportunity to do what they do best every day at work %
World	**26**	**47**
Latin America	44	60
U.S./Canada	39	53
Sub-Saharan Africa	33	52
Southeast Asia	26	48
South Asia	22	45
Western Europe	27	45
Post-Soviet Eurasia	25	41
Australia/ New Zealand	22	38
East Asia	17	35
Eastern Europe	19	35
Middle East/ North Africa	20	30

STRENGTHS-BASED TEAMS ARE MORE COLLABORATIVE AND COHESIVE

The benefits of a strengths-based culture are realized not only at the level of individual employees, but also in the interactions among team members. The best managers assemble teams strategically with a forensic eye for employees' individual and collective strengths. These managers are proactive in their selections and avoid assigning teams based solely on team members' availability. Knowing their team members' strengths, talented managers can set more targeted goals and maximize collaboration and productivity.

Team members who know each other's strengths can more effectively relate to one another, avoiding potential conflicts and boosting group cohesion. Gallup analysts recently conducted a study of 11,441 teams in six organizations where at least 30% of employees had completed the CliftonStrengths assessment. They determined that team members' awareness of their own strengths — and each other's — more strongly related to higher engagement and performance than did the specific composition of strengths on the team.

A STRENGTHS FOCUS CAN HELP WORKERS STAY ANCHORED IN TURBULENT TIMES

Strengths-based cultures transform organizations and promote adaptability and resilience — qualities that are increasingly vital in labor markets around the world. A strengths foundation that includes coaching and development gives people a greater sense of confidence in their abilities — a sense of their "true north" that helps them stay oriented for high productivity amid shifting workplace needs.

Gallup's work with businesses facing rapid changes brought about by external factors like mergers or technological disruption demonstrates how focusing on team members' strengths can help maintain and even boost their engagement through such challenging times. Strengths-based management can also help better position businesses for organic growth by identifying natural innovators within their workforces, as well as entrepreneurial-minded employees who can carry new ideas to fruition.

Beyond helping businesses establish strengths-based cultures, Gallup has in recent years been working with state and national governments to implement large-scale strengths programs that increase well-being and productivity among entire populations. If entire countries commit to exploring strengths and empowering people to be and do their best every day, the potential for economic and individual development is unlimited.

Empowering People to Succeed With the CliftonStrengths Assessment

Don Clifton's seminal work on strengths psychology led to the development of the CliftonStrengths assessment, an online tool that identifies a person's natural talents within a framework of 34 themes. By revealing how individuals most naturally think, feel and behave, the assessment helps employees understand and build on the unique areas in which they have the most potential to grow and succeed.

The instrument is at the heart of a global strengths movement that addresses the untapped potential of individuals and workgroups. By mid-2017, nearly 17 million people around the globe had taken the CliftonStrengths assessment across 22 different languages. See the appendix for a breakdown of assessment use by language.

What Does It Mean to Be a Strengths-Based Organization?

Some of the world's most progressive companies have embraced the goal of creating a strengths-based workplace. These companies target the entire workforce — leaders, managers and employees — and create systems, policies and procedures that support their strengths philosophy. As a result, these companies realize greater gains in their business outcomes than do those that take a less holistic approach to building a strengths-based culture.

Gallup has studied the world's leading strengths-based companies and discovered that they share compelling similarities. They have a mutual philosophy that highlights the value of a strengths-based culture, and they pursue that culture through four powerful strategies:

1. **Leadership:** Aligning the culture in a common language of strengths, disseminated through companywide management practices and communication. Some organizations designate a group of on-the-ground strengths champions who support managers and teams in their efforts to build a strengths-based culture.

2. **Empowerment:** Educating employees on the foundation of strengths and enabling them to make contributions beyond their title, role or job description.

3. **Engagement:** Generating excitement and enthusiasm for strengths-based teams by fostering environments that celebrate diversity and teamwork.

4. **Development:** Reorienting performance management systems to evaluate, reward and develop employees based on what they do best. Managers use individualized coaching focused on each employee's greatest opportunities for growth.

Systematically implementing strategies like these to attain a strengths-based culture can dramatically boost key business outcomes. In one company, stores that coupled a new customer strategy with a strengths-based focus generated an estimated 66% higher sales growth than the average store, versus 26% higher among those that executed the new customer strategy alone.

Team members who know each other's strengths can more effectively relate to one another, avoiding potential conflicts and boosting group cohesion.

04

Tapping Entrepreneurial Energy for Job Growth

63

23%

*of adults worldwide say they
have access to training on how
to start or grow a business.*

UNEMPLOYMENT, LOW-QUALITY JOBS AND INSTABILITY stifle progress in countries trying to build economic momentum. A vicious cycle perpetuates: Political instability and violence create risk, discouraging investment and job creation, which, in turn, fosters more instability — particularly among young people. This cycle can be a crippling problem in developing regions like sub-Saharan Africa, as well as more economically developed countries like Spain and Portugal.

Societies grappling with low growth rates and a scarcity of good jobs need ways to identify, nurture and empower high-growth "builders" — individuals who are engaged in the process of building something that creates new economic energy. Importantly, this group includes both those who start new businesses and those within existing organizations who develop products and services to address new market needs. In short, builders turn new ideas into value for customers.

> *Societies grappling with low growth rates and a scarcity of good jobs need ways to identify, nurture and empower high-growth "builders."*

Policymakers worldwide recognize that nurturing builders is essential to combat joblessness, reduce socio-economic disparities and spur overall economic growth. Many governments pursue a range of policies, from tax breaks or subsidized lending to training in finance, accounting and marketing to encourage individuals to start businesses. In most cases, however, such measures are not enough to encourage novel and high-growth startup activity — the kind that contributes to job creation and economic growth in a significant way.

Though most global leaders recognize the value of entrepreneurial activity, there is an urgent need to heighten residents' interest in the concept of entrepreneurship to ensure that those with the capacity to be powerful builders can aspire to fulfill that potential. At the societal level, that means taking concrete steps to help mitigate the risk that prospective business owners face by strengthening the rule of law, combating corruption and maintaining a social safety net that makes the consequences of failure less severe.

At the business level, leaders can directly address the need for increased entrepreneurial activity through a greater understanding of the personal characteristics that promote business-building success — and the strategies for equipping young people who display such talents with the knowledge and skills they need to create thriving enterprises.

THE MACRO VIEW: CULTURAL AND STRUCTURAL CHALLENGES

Entrepreneurial success that leads to job creation is harder to attain in some countries and regions than in others. Barriers may include deeply entrenched cultural or historical patterns. For example, in developed Western countries with free markets, people are far more likely to say they would rather work for a private business than for the government. However, where residents are accustomed to a more paternalistic relationship between citizens and the state — as is the case in much of the Middle East/North Africa and post-Soviet Eurasia — people commonly prefer to have a job working for the government.

PREFERENCES OF WORKING FOR GOVERNMENT VERSUS
PRIVATE BUSINESS

Would you rather have a job working for the government or working for a business?

■ % Government   ■ % Business

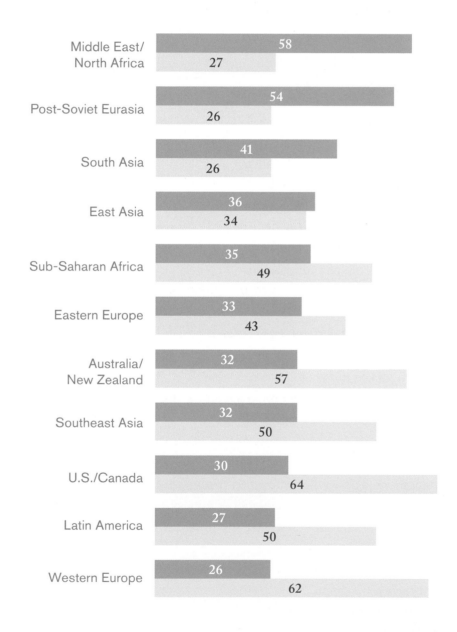

Region	% Government	% Business
Middle East/North Africa	58	27
Post-Soviet Eurasia	54	26
South Asia	41	26
East Asia	36	34
Sub-Saharan Africa	35	49
Eastern Europe	33	43
Australia/New Zealand	32	57
Southeast Asia	32	50
U.S./Canada	30	64
Latin America	27	50
Western Europe	26	62

These data demonstrate the influence that cultural factors have on residents' likelihood to consider starting a business. In regions where risk aversion is part of the cultural fabric, or where individual initiative is downplayed in favor of a more collective mindset, fewer people may even consider starting their own business. To stimulate entrepreneurial activity, governments and businesses in these countries need to identify and counter cultural factors that may be hindering innovation.

Unfortunately, cultural biases against business startups are often reinforced by government policies that do not encourage private-sector growth, such as burdensome regulations for registering businesses or obtaining credit. Further, many countries lack institutional support for developing the human capital necessary to meet the needs of growing businesses, such as equitable education and healthcare systems.

Many countries lack institutional support for developing the human capital necessary to meet the needs of growing businesses, such as equitable education and healthcare systems.

In most regions, including economically developed areas like Western Europe and the U.S./Canada, less than one-third of residents believe that their government makes it easy to start a business, implying that public investment in education and healthcare may not be contributing to private-sector growth as effectively as it could be.

In other countries — most notably, sub-Saharan Africa — support for human capital development is so weak that even in places where governments make it easy to start a business, the vast majority of entrepreneurs do not have the skills needed to launch startups that have the potential for long-term growth.

The following table ranks global regions by the average "yes" responses to these factors, revealing that public perceptions of these items are most positive in Southeast Asia, currently one of the most economically dynamic regions in the world.

VIEWS OF LOCAL FACTORS THAT HELP TRANSFORM HUMAN CAPITAL INTO
BUSINESS DEVELOPMENT

	Believe government makes it easy to start a business* %	Satisfied with local education system %	Satisfied with local access to healthcare %	Average index %
Southeast Asia	49	82	77	69
Australia/ New Zealand	25	70	84	60
U.S./Canada	30	65	75	57
South Asia	34	73	60	56
Western Europe	25	66	75	55
East Asia	24	59	70	51
Sub-Saharan Africa	36	54	43	44
Latin America	30	57	42	43
Middle East/ North Africa	28	49	49	42
Eastern Europe	14	59	51	41
Post-Soviet Eurasia	18	54	40	37

*Data for this question collected in 2013, except in South Asia, Southeast Asia and Australia/New Zealand where it was collected in 2014.

In addition to establishing critical supports for business development, Gallup's global data suggest that leaders in some regions need to highlight the critical role of business builders in economic progress. One advantage characteristic of the United States is that its successful entrepreneurs are highly respected, even held up as emblematic of the American ideal. In many countries — particularly those with low social mobility and pervasive corruption — business owners are less likely to be admired.

Gallup polls conducted in 2013 asked respondents worldwide whether those who run their own business are good role models for youth in their country. The proportion who said "yes" ranged from 88% in the U.S./Canada to less than half (46%) in Eastern Europe and post-Soviet Eurasia.

PERCEPTION OF BUSINESS OWNERS AS ROLE MODELS

In [country], are people who run their own business considered good role models for youth, or not?

% Yes

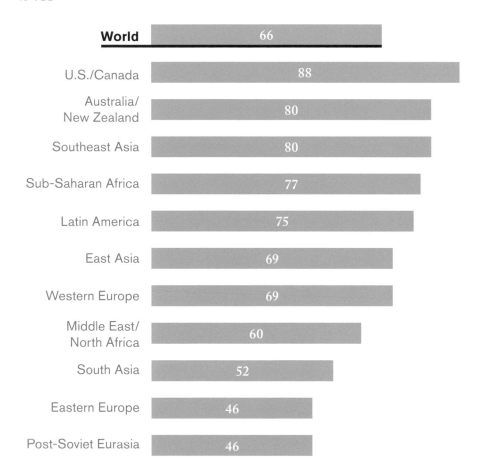

World	66
U.S./Canada	88
Australia/New Zealand	80
Southeast Asia	80
Sub-Saharan Africa	77
Latin America	75
East Asia	69
Western Europe	69
Middle East/North Africa	60
South Asia	52
Eastern Europe	46
Post-Soviet Eurasia	46

THE MICRO VIEW: NURTURING TALENTED ENTREPRENEURS TO SPUR ORGANIC GROWTH

More than anything else, generating enthusiasm for entrepreneurship depends on taking steps to increase entrepreneurs' odds of success. In addition to high-level efforts to improve the institutional environment in which small and medium-sized enterprises (SMEs) operate, smaller-scale initiatives such as business incubators and entrepreneurial training are essential. In many places, opportunities to attain the basic knowledge required to start and grow a business are relatively scarce, presenting a major barrier to SME development. Worldwide, 23% of adults say they have access to such training; regionally, only in the U.S./Canada and Australia/New Zealand do most residents say they have access.

AVAILABILITY OF TRAINING ON STARTING OR GROWING A BUSINESS

Do you have access to training on how to start or grow a business, or not?

% Yes

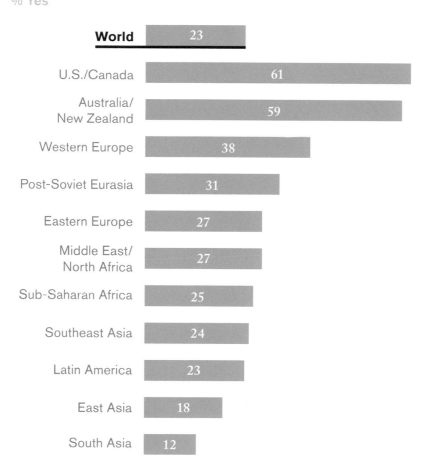

World	23
U.S./Canada	61
Australia/New Zealand	59
Western Europe	38
Post-Soviet Eurasia	31
Eastern Europe	27
Middle East/North Africa	27
Sub-Saharan Africa	25
Southeast Asia	24
Latin America	23
East Asia	18
South Asia	12

Tools for identifying and developing innate "builder" talent can further bolster efforts to promote entrepreneurial success. Builders, particularly those who introduce new products or services, are often confronted with formidable challenges. They typically must navigate untested markets, working in uncertain environments with limited resources and no guarantee of success. Thus, personality characteristics such as risk tolerance, achievement drive, creativity and self-efficacy are important to success.

Identifying and supporting individuals who have such characteristics can spur high-growth venture creation. Gallup's research indicates that training innately talented builders to understand their own traits, attitudes and values leads to psychological clarity through which they gain confidence in their ability to start and grow new ventures.

Gallup's research indicates that training innately talented builders to understand their own traits, attitudes and values leads to psychological clarity through which they gain confidence in their ability to start and grow new ventures.

Gallup has developed a structured online assessment called the Builder Profile 10™ (BP10) with the goal of identifying and developing builder talent. The assessment was derived from a study of success among 4,000 entrepreneurs in the U.S., Germany and Mexico. The results identified 10 talents that were most highly correlated with business success. Successful builders use some mix of these characteristics in starting or growing new enterprises:

- **Confidence:** You accurately know yourself and understand others.

- **Delegator:** You recognize that you cannot do everything and are willing to contemplate a shift in style and control.

- **Determination:** You persevere through difficult, even seemingly insurmountable, obstacles.

- **Disruptor:** You exhibit creativity in taking an existing idea or product and turning it into something better.

- **Independent:** You are prepared to do whatever needs to be done to build a successful venture.

- **Knowledge:** You constantly search for information that is relevant to growing your business.

- **Profitability:** You make decisions based on observed or anticipated effect on profit.

- **Relationship:** You have high social awareness and an ability to build relationships that are beneficial for the firm's survival and growth.

- **Risk:** You instinctively know how to manage high-risk situations.

- **Selling:** You are the best spokesperson for the business.

The social and cultural dynamics that affect interest in entrepreneurial activity play out within organizations as well — and their implications for business growth may be just as important. As startups begin to grow, they eventually face the same issues that existing companies face: the need for innovation. But in countries with a tradition of strong central authority, like many former Soviet republics, employees' entrepreneurial and innovative impulses are suppressed. Thus, processes for identifying and developing natural builders can also be invaluable for spurring "intrapreneurship" — the implementation of new ideas and products within organizations — to help businesses stay well-positioned for future market needs.

Processes for identifying and developing natural builders can also be invaluable for spurring "intrapreneurship" — the implementation of new ideas and products within organizations — to help businesses stay well-positioned for future market needs.

PUBLIC- AND PRIVATE-SECTOR LEADERS CAN TOGETHER BUILD THRIVING ENTREPRENEURIAL ECOSYSTEMS

When government and private-sector organizations collaborate to promote entrepreneurial activity, they can address the task at several levels, from the macro public policy environment to individual students and employees.

Mexico is one country involved in pursuing such collaborative strategies. Since 2014, Gallup has been working with Mexico's Ministry of Economic Development, the Ministry of Education and several public high school systems in Mexico City to identify and develop future entrepreneurs. These students gain self-confidence and motivation — essential attributes for entrepreneurs. And even if they aren't ready to start their own business right away, the seed has been planted, producing the potential to grow in the future.

Identifying entrepreneurs and providing them with training and support helps them realize that a successful business startup is a viable option — one that increases their economic potential. A majority may not ever start their own business, but training them to think like entrepreneurs makes them better prepared to work in uncertain and changing environments. Over the long term, such strategies for developing talented builders can help community leaders cultivate a broader entrepreneurial ecosystem that leads to more business startups and higher success rates.

When government and private-sector organizations collaborate to promote entrepreneurial activity, they can address the task at several levels, from the macro public policy environment to individual students and employees.

05

Western Europe

Austria, Belgium, Denmark, Finland, France, Germany, Iceland, Ireland, Italy, Luxembourg, Malta, Netherlands, Norway, Portugal, Spain, Sweden, Switzerland, United Kingdom

10%

of employees in Western Europe are engaged.

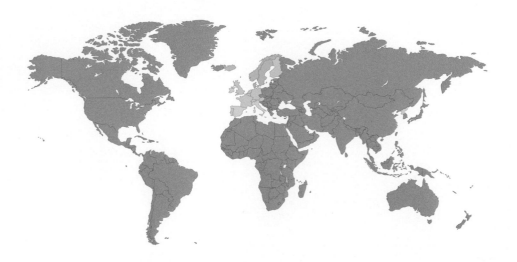

% Employed full time
for an employer

36%   67%
Italy   Sweden

See the appendix for "good jobs" data, by country.

46%

of working–age adults in Germany are employed full time for an employer.

vs.

32%

globally

WESTERN EUROPE IS ONE OF the most socially and economically developed regions in the world, but many of its countries have endured financial and political turmoil over the last decade. The global recession of 2009 triggered debt crises in several countries, including Portugal, Ireland and Spain, sending shock waves throughout the European Union. Much of Western Europe is still plagued by high unemployment and slow growth.

Discrepancies in workforce productivity have driven much of the resulting political fallout. Workers in debt-ridden southern EU countries tend to contribute much less to their country's gross domestic product (GDP) with every hour worked than do workers in many northern nations, such as Germany and the Scandinavian countries. The consequence is that more solvent EU countries have had to bail out those on the verge of economic catastrophe — contributing to the current debate about the future of European integration.

Western Europe is one of the most socially and economically developed regions in the world, but many of its countries have endured financial and political turmoil over the last decade.

Employment data from the Gallup World Polls conducted from 2014 to 2016 indicate that northern countries in Western Europe tend to have higher rates of residents working full time for an employer — a key metric in assessing the maturity and vitality of a country's labor market. The Scandinavian countries top the list — particularly Sweden, where two-thirds of residents aged 23 to 65 (67%) work full time for an employer. This number falls below 40% in Spain (37%) and Italy (36%).

In some cases, however, focusing exclusively on this employment metric may give a misleading picture of labor markets in the region. In Germany, for example, less than half of working-age adults (46%) are employed full time for an employer, but relatively high proportions are employed part time by choice (15%) or are self-employed (10%). In a developed economy like Germany's, such responses likely reflect flexibility in employment options to accommodate work-life balance.

EMPLOYEE ENGAGEMENT CONSISTENTLY LOW ACROSS WESTERN EUROPE

Variations within the EU notwithstanding, some issues affecting Western Europe's workforces are overarching. One challenge common in highly developed countries around the world is an aging population: Low birth rates and rising life expectancies mean older residents are retiring at a more rapid rate than younger residents are entering the workforce.

But there is another challenge: Throughout Western Europe, employee engagement levels are relatively low. Regionally, just 10% of employed residents are engaged — involved in and enthusiastic about their work. By comparison, 33% of employees in the U.S. are engaged.

Atop the list of Western European countries is Norway, with 17% of employees engaged in their work. As dismal as that percentage seems, in some countries, it is far lower. In France, for example, just 6% of employees are engaged, while 25% are actively disengaged. In Italy, 5% are engaged, and 30% are actively disengaged — the highest proportion of actively disengaged employees in all 155 populations worldwide included in this analysis.

These dismal engagement results offer insight into why labor productivity in many European countries trails that in the U.S. and in most cases has not returned to the growth rates seen before the global financial crisis. Europe's businesses need new ways to address these productivity challenges so they can move past the malaise that weighs many of them down.

The good news is that they often need to look no further than their own workforces. That's not to say that addressing challenges like these is easy — it typically requires a cultural transformation that affects how all employees think about their job and interact with those around them. It also means committing to management changes that drive continual development, positivity and future orientation. But such transformation is entirely possible and offers a powerful competitive advantage, as industry leaders on both sides of the Atlantic have demonstrated.

ENGAGEMENT LOW, ACTIVE DISENGAGEMENT HIGH AMONG EMPLOYEES IN SEVERAL WESTERN EUROPEAN COUNTRIES

	Engaged %	Not engaged %	Actively disengaged %
Norway	17	75	8
Denmark	16	73	11
Iceland	16	76	8
Malta	16	70	14
Portugal	16	70	14
Germany	15	70	15
Sweden	14	75	11
Ireland	13	71	16
Switzerland	13	76	12
Austria	12	71	18
Finland	12	76	12
Netherlands	12	75	13
United Kingdom	11	68	21
Belgium	10	73	17
Luxembourg	8	80	13
France	6	69	25
Spain	6	79	15
Italy	5	64	30

WESTERN EUROPE SPOTLIGHT: EMPLOYEE PRODUCTIVITY IN EUROPE VERSUS THE U.S.

Europe can match U.S. productivity if it puts greater emphasis on people management.

Gallup's current workplace results from European employees don't make for pleasant reading for the continent's employers. Most employees feel underused and unable to be their best at work. Levels of engagement have been low for the best part of a decade in Europe. If those trends don't change, European countries' productivity levels will continue to lag behind those in the U.S. And given that some of Europe's largest economies are facing aging populations without enough young workers to replace their rapidly rising number of retirees, the potential exists for the gap in productivity to widen.

This article places Gallup's workplace engagement data (based on Gallup World Polls conducted from 2014 to 2016) alongside other high-profile indicators of workforce vitality, including:

- global competitiveness (World Economic Forum [WEF], 2016-2017)

- country-level data for productivity and hours worked (Organisation for Economic Cooperation and Development [OECD], 2015)

- global creativity (Martin Prosperity Institute, University of Toronto, Rotman School of Management, 2015)

To understand what facilitates productivity, Gallup placed a country's GDP per capita in the context of its performance on several WEF indicators of productivity and long-term prosperity, such as health, education, infrastructure and innovation. Our analysis shows that these indicators — the strongest being technological readiness — account for about 89% of the variation in GDP per capita among 34 OECD countries. Gallup's work with clients in the U.S. and Europe leads us to believe that the remaining 11% of variation hinges on how people are managed in the workplace.

Higher engagement means greater productivity. Gallup research shows that, across industries and countries, teams with highly engaged members are, on average, 17% more productive than those with lower average engagement. Levels of engagement have been growing slowly but steadily in the U.S.; 33% of American workers are engaged versus only 10% in Western Europe.

Consider this analogy for engagement: On one side of a rope in a 10-person tug-of-war competition, a team from the U.S. has three fully engaged people working hard to pull their team over the line. On the other side, one European is engaged in the contest, weighed down with nine teammates who haven't been equipped to put in their best effort. Assuming the size, strengths and expertise of the tug-of-war teams are equivalent, which team would prevail?

Gallup research shows that, across industries and countries, teams with highly engaged members are, on average, 17% more productive than those with lower average engagement.

The World Economic Forum's Basic Requirements Subindex — the component of the WEF's Global Competitiveness Index that compiles basic indicators related to institutions, infrastructure, macroeconomic environment, and health and primary education — ranks Germany 10th in the world, and the U.S. comes in at 27th. Nevertheless, American workers outperform their German counterparts. German workers are productive and creative relative to most other countries studied, according to data from the OECD and Martin Prosperity Institute, respectively — but they aren't engaged at work. Compared with the Germans, U.S. employees are far more likely to be engaged. In fact, among all OECD countries with relatively high productivity and creativity scores, the U.S. has the highest proportion of engaged employees.

PRODUCTIVITY, CREATIVITY AND ENGAGEMENT AMONG OECD WORKFORCES

% Employees engaged at work

- ▪ 5
- ■ 10
- ■ 15
- ■ 20
- ■ 25+

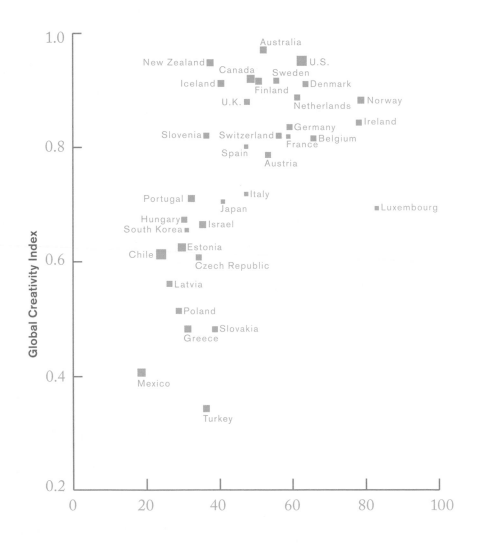

2015 GDP Per Hour Worked

Sum of 2015 GDP per hour worked vs. sum of Global Creativity Index. Size shows percentage of employees engaged at work.

Previous generations and governments have bequeathed Western Europeans with what should be unassailable productivity advantages: universal healthcare, decent schools, technical training and apprenticeships, good public transport and roads, and a welfare safety net — but European companies are letting down their workers. The Nordic countries — Switzerland, Germany, Holland, Austria, Belgium, France, Luxembourg — and, to a lesser degree, the U.K., lead the U.S. in these productivity enablers. Despite this, U.S. companies are out-managing their European counterparts, resulting in much higher proportions of engaged employees.

In 2016, the 10 most valuable publicly traded companies in the world were all from the U.S. — four of the 10 didn't exist 50 years ago, three didn't exist 25 years ago and one is just 13 years old. Three of the four hyperdynamic companies have reputations as being progressive, outstanding places to work. By contrast, it's hard to think of large European companies where the reasons people want to join go beyond salary, benefits packages and the potential for progression — and include *an engaging culture*.

In our organizational work, we're often struck by how little stock European management teams put into leading their people — despite survey after survey showing that good management and leadership are by far the strongest drivers of how engaged people are. Consequently, inept managers pervade many European companies at all levels. It's a shame: Driving higher productivity through better engagement is fast and inexpensive compared with, say, overhauling a national health system or upgrading public transport.

WESTERN EUROPE SPOTLIGHT: UNITED KINGDOM

Breaking up is hard to do — employee engagement suffers amid post-Brexit uncertainty.

"Panic on the streets of London, panic on the streets of Birmingham." So sang Britain's foremost miserablist Morrissey on The Smiths' song "Panic" in 1986. Thirty years later, in the wake of the United Kingdom's decision to leave the European Union, there are many who would paint the country's future in a similar light. Given that it is unprecedented for a country to leave the EU, there is no historical record to help predict what happens next. The resulting uncertainty may leave many British employees — particularly those in export-oriented industries — worried about what the future will bring.

11%

of British workers are engaged at work.

Gallup's latest workplace data reveal that, when it comes to employee engagement, neither the average British company nor those in many mainland European countries can afford much of a decline. Only about one in 10 British workers (11%) is engaged at work, while the majority (68%) are not engaged, and two in 10 (21%) are actively disengaged. Aggregated results for the EU overall are similar.

EMPLOYEE ENGAGEMENT IN THE U.K. AND EU

	Engaged %	Not engaged %	Actively disengaged %
United Kingdom	11	68	21
European Union overall	11	70	19

The relationship between employee engagement and positive business outcomes is described in more detail in Chapter 2, but here, it suffices to note that engaged workgroups are 17% more productive than are workgroups in the bottom quartile of engagement. With the United Kingdom's annual GDP growth rate not having strayed far from 2% recently, an uptick in productivity would be a huge boost for an area newly shorn of the protection of the EU single market. In terms of GDP per working hour, the U.K. currently lags behind many developed countries — including the U.S., by about 30 percentage points.

The Millennial Factor

While the U.K.'s economy could benefit from a boost, preparing for the future in an uncertain environment is never easy. Among the most important considerations for company leadership are the needs and preferences of a growing sector of the U.K.'s employee and consumer populations: the millennial generation.

To some extent, knowing what millennials want as customers and as employees will determine whether a company succeeds over the next 20 years. Gallup's research on millennial employees in the U.K. and Europe suggests that they are unforgiving of tragic workplaces and managers. Even with sky-high unemployment, little disposable income and minimal savings, millennials will leave a job that they feel stunts their growth. The flip side is that these are exactly the type of fearless, status quo-rejecting people that companies need to stay relevant.

What's more is that 75% of 18- to 24-year-olds in Britain voted to remain a part of the EU in the referendum. Many of the country's young adults feel betrayed by their elders' vote to seemingly limit their future and freedom of mobility. It is going to take more than fancy sofas at Google's London headquarters in Soho to win back millennials' allegiance. Businesses need to understand the attitudes and aspirations that motivate them.

However, many British businesses currently neglect motivational considerations when it comes to younger employees — or those of any age. At best, leaders in such businesses think their people are important, but they either don't know what to do, or their thinking around how to raise performance is plain wrong. At worst, they don't consider people as a factor in how they win.

75%

of 18- to 24-year-olds in Britain voted to remain a part of the EU in the referendum.

Businesses Need to Lead in Times of Uncertainty

While uncertainty reigns over the United Kingdom, with the daunting tasks of renegotiating trade deals with the rest of the world, rewriting laws that are no longer applicable and keeping skittish international investors from bolting to continental Europe, it is business leaders who can provide stability for their employees.

The first key is to communicate. Businesses need to be upfront and clear in their messaging, especially when delivering bad news. It is possible to deliver difficult news without disengaging employees. If a company has recently undergone job losses, pay cuts and reduced market share, leaders don't need to hire motivational speakers, but they do need to deliver messages infused with trust, stability, compassion and hope for employees. On a local level, company culture should call for managers to communicate expectations clearly and listen to and value the opinions of their employees. No one wants to feel like they are ignored.

Secondly, there must be individualization, especially with millennials in mind. Their interests are so diverse and wide-ranging that a one-size-fits-all approach will be ineffective and possibly even counter-productive. For employees to thrive and be engaged, they need to be in positions where they can do their best work every day, know and use their strengths, and have frequent check-ins with their manager and mentors to reinforce positive behavior.

Recognition is the final piece of the puzzle. Effective, individualized communication has a restorative effect on employees, and the effect of a well-timed, meaningful piece of recognition can be a huge motivational boost. It is important to balance negative messages with positive ones and to look for the silver lining: Connect what you are asking of your employees back to your organization's mission. Let them know how they are contributing to a greater purpose. There is a popular notion that millennials don't like to work, but that notion is a myth. They just need to be motivated properly.

> *Effective, individualized communication has a restorative effect on employees, and the effect of a well-timed, meaningful piece of recognition can be a huge motivational boost.*

With the British government sailing into uncharted waters as Brexit negotiations proceed, it is up to businesses to provide the stability that employees are looking for. Business leaders need to have the right mindset and skills to make sure their employees are engaged at work. With so much at stake, one thing is certain: "Keep calm and carry on" is no longer the panacea it once was.

WESTERN EUROPE SPOTLIGHT: GERMANY

German companies need new workplace strategies to boost retention and ensure work-life balance.

Germany has long been recognized as the economic powerhouse of Europe. However, Gallup's workplace studies indicate that only 15% of employees in the country are engaged at work (emotionally and behaviorally connected to their job and their company's mission), leaving much room for improvement. Though this figure is in line with Western Europe (10% engaged regionally), it is less than half of the percentage in countries where employee engagement levels are highest, including the U.S., at 33%.

Another 15% of German employees are actively disengaged, meaning that for every employee who is highly motivated, positive and productive, another is resentful and disruptive. Gallup estimates that disengaged German workers cost the country's economy between 80.3 and 105.1 billion euros each year — for example, through higher annual absentee rates (10.3 days for actively disengaged employees, compared with 6.5 days for engaged workers) or customer-facing employees who transfer their negativity to consumers.

80.3-105.1

Gallup estimates that 80.3-105.1 billion euros are lost each year due to disengaged German workers.

Job Security and Work-Life Balance Top the List of Employees' Expectations

Engaging workers means not just ensuring that they know what is expected of them, but also understanding what they expect from their job. When German employees are asked to rate the importance of 19 possible employment attributes on a 1-5 scale, work-life balance ties with job security for the highest average rating. Thus, while German workers need stability in uncertain economic times, they also want to know that their job will fit well into their life.

GERMAN EMPLOYEES RATE JOB SECURITY, WORK-LIFE BALANCE AS MOST IMPORTANT EMPLOYER ATTRIBUTES

Average rating on 1-5 scale, with 1 being "not at all important" and 5 being "extremely important"

	Importance
Job security	4.52
Work-life balance and personal well-being	4.52
Doing what I am really good at	4.45
Great colleagues to work with	4.44
Great manager	4.35
Vacation days	4.33
Challenges and excitements	4.31
Flexibility in working hours/time	4.15
Autonomy	4.13
Income or income potential	4.12
The organization's culture	4.02
The organization and its leaders' reputation	4.00
Benefits, perks, convenience	3.96
The organization's mission and purpose	3.92
Innovation	3.85
Professional or career growth and development opportunities	3.79
Health and well-being programs	3.69
Opportunity to manage or lead others	3.68
Child care	3.05

The good news is that German employers seem to have made some progress in this regard. In 2005, one-quarter of employees (25%) strongly agreed with the statement "My company allows me to balance work and private life" — 37% strongly agree today. However, there is still a substantial gap between the perceived importance of this expectation and workers' satisfaction with how well employers are meeting it.

It's not that Germans don't see work as an important part of their life — in fact, their work ethic is so strong that more than three-quarters of employees (77%) say they would continue to work even if they inherited enough money to make working unnecessary. However, working consistently long hours in a job that offers little flexibility can lead to burnout and associated consequences: exhaustion, irritability, physical ailments, and suffering relationships with friends and family.

Of actively disengaged German workers, 53% say they felt burned out at work in the past 30 days, but only 17% of engaged employees report having the same feelings. German leaders need to recognize burnout not as just a psychological problem, but as a serious economic one as well — burnout costs businesses 9 billion euros each year.

77%

of German employees say they would continue to work even if they inherited enough money to make working unnecessary.

Meeting Employees' Expectations Is a Manager's No. 1 Job

Creating a culture of enthusiasm, energy and positivity should be at the very top of every manager's to-do list. To accomplish this, managers must have ongoing conversations with employees in addition to formal performance evaluations so they better understand the factors affecting their team members' performance and can work with them on ways to ensure work-life conflicts don't erode their engagement or productivity levels.

Having a "great manager" is also among the five workplace qualities that German employees rate as most important. Almost one in five German workers (18%) say they have considered leaving their current job within the past year solely because of a bad manager. That figure drops to just 3% among engaged employees, whereas nearly half of actively disengaged employees (45%) have considered leaving because of a bad manager.

Having a "great manager" is among the five workplace qualities that German employees rate as most important.

3%

of engaged employees have considered leaving because of a bad manager.

VS.

45%

of actively disengaged employees have considered leaving because of a bad manager.

Despite the need for these critical relationships, German management culture is often sorely lacking training or education that emphasizes managing people; instead, it remains largely focused on administrative processes and finances. In many cases, MBA programs and human resources practices continue to give short shrift to psychological factors affecting motivation and productivity among the workers who drive Germany's robust economy.

By contrast, managers who are skilled at engaging employees think of themselves as coaches and mentors who nurture workforce talent. They take a more holistic view of employees' work experiences — seeking common ground between employees' personal goals and the needs of the organization so that the two can grow together into the future. Managers who have ongoing training about how to approach their job as a coach and who understand how to engage employees could go a long way in creating a more energetic, productive and happy German workforce.

Managers who are skilled at engaging employees take a more holistic view of employees' work experiences — seeking common ground between employees' personal goals and the needs of the organization so that the two can grow together into the future.

06

Eastern Europe

Albania, Bosnia and Herzegovina, Bulgaria, Croatia, Cyprus, Czech Republic, Estonia, Greece, Hungary, Kosovo, Latvia, Lithuania, Macedonia, Montenegro, Northern Cyprus, Poland, Romania, Serbia, Slovakia, Slovenia

15%

of employees in
Eastern Europe
are engaged.

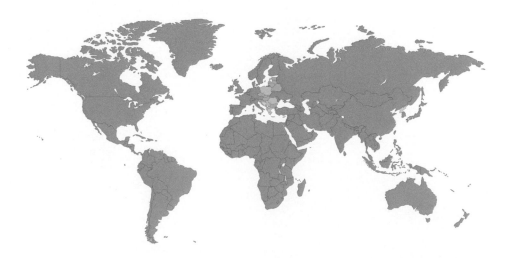

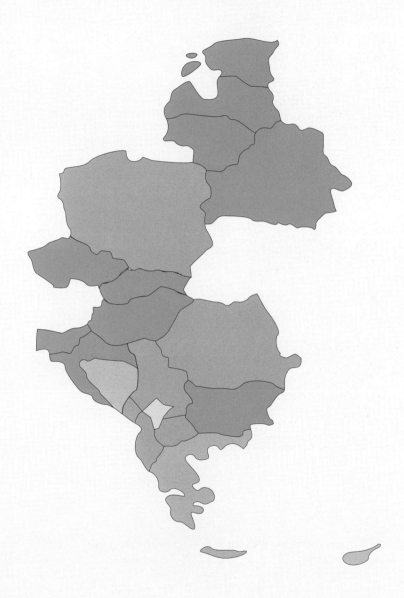

% Employed full time
for an employer

19%
Albania

66%
Estonia

See the appendix for "good jobs" data, by country.

24%

*of Eastern European residents
would like to move permanently
to another country, given
the opportunity.*

vs.

14%

globally

PRIOR TO THE FINANCIAL CRISIS that sent the global economy reeling in 2009, many Eastern European countries were seeing rapid economic growth. Most had come through a chaotic period of privatization and labor market reform after the fall of the Soviet Union and were reaping the benefits, including substantial foreign direct investment. In much of the region, however, economic growth rates have still not recovered, partly because global investors remain more risk-averse than they were before the crisis.

The investment boom in many transitional countries of Eastern Europe — similar to the global commodity boom in Latin America and sub-Saharan Africa — ended around 2013 when China's growth began to decelerate. In both cases, the source of growth proved unsustainable, vulnerable to changes in global demand that are difficult to predict and impossible to control.

Eastern Europe faces the challenge of generating more reliable, organic sources of growth — most critically, by retaining and developing its human capital.

As in other developing regions, Eastern Europe faces the challenge of generating more reliable, organic sources of growth — most critically, by retaining and developing its human capital. Many countries in the region urgently need to stem the flow of emigrants to the West. A 2016 report from the International Monetary Fund noted that "Emigration from Central, Eastern and Southeastern Europe has been unusually large, persistent and dominated by educated and young people." The report goes on to discuss the crippling effects on public finances and private-sector development.

Overall, 24% of Eastern European residents tell Gallup that, given the opportunity, they would like to move permanently to another country — a regional figure exceeded only by sub-Saharan Africa at 31% (though results from Latin America and the Middle East/North Africa are similar to those from Eastern Europe). Among Eastern Europeans with at least four years of higher education, the proportion who would prefer to emigrate is similar, at 23%, but it surges to 41% among residents aged 15 to 29. Eight in 10 young adults in Albania (79%) say they would like to emigrate, as do 62% in Bosnia and Herzegovina and 54% in Slovenia.

YOUNG RESIDENTS MORE LIKELY THAN OVERALL EASTERN EUROPEAN POPULATIONS TO WANT TO EMIGRATE

% Would prefer to move permanently to another country

	All residents %	Residents aged 15-29 %	Gap (pct. pts.)
Slovenia	27	54	27
Bosnia and Herzegovina	39	62	23
Lithuania	25	48	23
Serbia	26	49	23
Estonia	22	43	21
Hungary	20	41	21
Albania	59	79	20
Bulgaria	21	40	19
Romania	27	45	18
Montenegro	27	44	17
Latvia	16	32	16
Macedonia	35	51	16
Croatia	18	33	15
Czech Republic	13	28	15
Greece	21	36	15
Slovakia	16	31	15
Poland	22	36	14
Cyprus	32	45	13
Northern Cyprus	27	40	13
Kosovo	39	47	8

At the heart of Eastern Europe's emigration problem may be the pervasive belief that hard work does not equate to advancement. Just 51% of Eastern Europeans overall agree that it is possible in their country to get ahead by working hard — easily the lowest regional proportion worldwide. The region's young people (those aged 15 to 29) are somewhat more likely than their elders to be optimistic in this regard, with 58% saying it is possible to get ahead by working hard; however, this is still one of the lowest proportions worldwide.

YOUNG RESIDENTS IN EASTERN EUROPE SLIGHTLY MORE LIKELY TO AGREE PEOPLE CAN GET AHEAD BY WORKING HARD

% Yes to "Can people in this country get ahead by working hard, or not?"

	All residents %	Residents aged 15-29 %	Gap (pct. pts.)
Eastern Europe	51	58	7
Post-Soviet Eurasia	60	67	7
U.S./Canada	82	88	6
Australia/ New Zealand	86	90	4
Latin America	78	80	2
South Asia	80	82	2
Middle East/ North Africa	77	78	1
Southeast Asia	88	89	1
Sub-Saharan Africa	86	86	-
Western Europe	78	78	-
East Asia	58	55	-3

Management practices that fail to give employees a sense of personal progress may also lead many to consider emigration. Gallup's national surveys find that just 15% of Eastern Europe's employed residents are engaged at work. Among those employees, a clear majority — 61% — say it is possible to get ahead by working hard, versus 52% of those who are not engaged and 34% of those who are actively disengaged.

15%

of Eastern Europe's employed residents are engaged at work.

The specific engagement indicator that Eastern European employees are least likely to rate positively is "There is someone at work who encourages my development." This finding points to a lack of focus on employees' future within their organization, which may lead them to envision a future elsewhere.

Despite the region's challenges, most Eastern European countries have advantages they can build on, including relatively well-educated populations, moderate labor costs and proximity to large consumer markets in Western Europe. However, those factors will mean little if Eastern European governments and employers cannot change young people's perception that, in their efforts to build a better future for themselves and their families, the region's workers are swimming against the tide.

Management practices that fail to give employees a sense of personal progress may lead many to consider emigration.

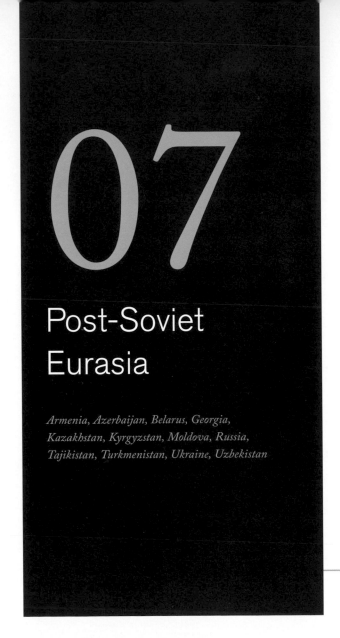

07

Post-Soviet Eurasia

*Armenia, Azerbaijan, Belarus, Georgia,
Kazakhstan, Kyrgyzstan, Moldova, Russia,
Tajikistan, Turkmenistan, Ukraine, Uzbekistan*

25%

of employees in
post-Soviet Eurasia
are engaged.

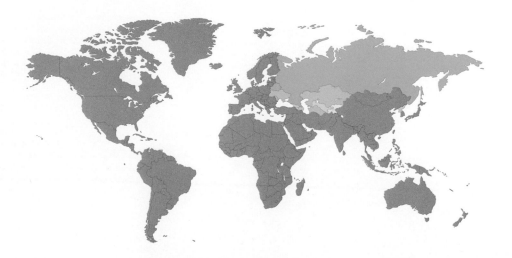

% Employed full time
for an employer

17%
Tajikistan

63%
Belarus

See the appendix for "good jobs" data, by country.

18%

of residents in post–Soviet Eurasia
say their government makes it
easy to start a business.

VS.

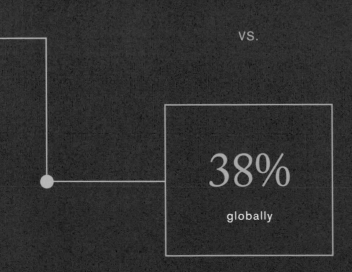

38%

globally

THE 15 COUNTRIES OF THE former Soviet Union went through a chaotic period following the USSR's collapse in 1991. Previously centralized industries and value chains were splintered, leading to capital flight, hyperinflation, rampant tax avoidance and a host of other problems. In the 2000s, however, most of these economies managed to rebound. For oil-exporting nations like Russia and Kazakhstan, high energy prices fueled healthy growth rates, while countries, such as the Baltic states, that had most successfully made democratic and market-oriented reforms became attractive targets for foreign direct investment.

In many former Soviet republics, however, this progress was interrupted by the global recession, which sharply reduced the flow of investment capital, and by China's slowing growth, which led to falling energy prices. In Russia, this resulted in a full-scale economic crisis and the collapse of the ruble in 2014. As in other regions, the economic turmoil highlighted the need to lay a new, more reliable foundation for economic progress based largely on the development and optimization of human talent.

That's a daunting prospect, however, for post-Soviet populations accustomed to highly centralized planning and unaccustomed to taking the initiatives necessary for entrepreneurial growth. Gallup finds that collectively, residents in these countries are about twice as likely to say they would rather have a job working for the government than for a business (54% vs. 26%, respectively). Further, along with East Asia, post-Soviet Eurasia is one of only two global regions in which less than half of residents say their local area is a good place to start a business.

Post–Soviet Eurasia is one of only two global regions in which less than half of residents say their local area is a good place to start a business.

LESS THAN MAJORITY OF POST-SOVIET EURASIA RESIDENTS BELIEVE THEIR AREA IS GOOD FOR STARTING NEW BUSINESSES

Is the city or area where you live a good place or not a good place to live for people starting new businesses?

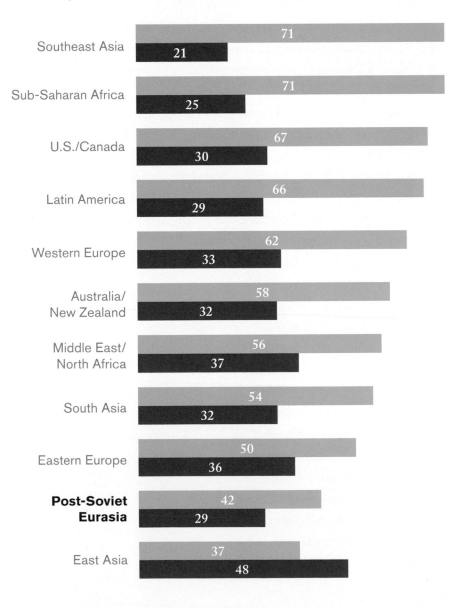

■ % Good place ■ % Not a good place

Region	% Good place	% Not a good place
Southeast Asia	71	21
Sub-Saharan Africa	71	25
U.S./Canada	67	30
Latin America	66	29
Western Europe	62	33
Australia/New Zealand	58	32
Middle East/North Africa	56	37
South Asia	54	32
Eastern Europe	50	36
Post-Soviet Eurasia	42	29
East Asia	37	48

The aversion to starting private-sector businesses is reinforced in many post-Soviet populations by the prevailing perception that government regulations and procedures will be barriers to entrepreneurship. Overall, just 18% of residents in post-Soviet Eurasia say their government makes it easy to start a business — one of the lowest figures among the 11 global regions studied.

Widespread corruption and lack of transparency are also hindrances, as they elevate the uncertainty and risks associated with starting businesses. Almost three-fourths of residents in post-Soviet countries (72%) have the perception that corruption is widespread in government, while two-thirds (67%) say it is widespread in business.

The aversion to starting private-sector businesses is reinforced in many post-Soviet populations by the prevailing perception that government regulations and procedures will be barriers to entrepreneurship.

Widespread corruption and lack of transparency are hindrances, as they elevate the uncertainty and risks associated with starting businesses.

72%
have a perception that corruption is widespread in government.

VS.

67%
have a perception that corruption is widespread in business.

The governments in post-Soviet countries have much work to do to combat bribery and other forms of endemic corruption and to change the perception that they are risky environments for business startups. The region's education systems can also play a significant role in changing widespread skepticism regarding entrepreneurship in two ways:

1. by placing greater emphasis on entrepreneurial training among curricular goals in secondary schools and universities

2. by focusing on self-discovery and strengths development in all educational strategies

Identifying and developing young people with the greatest potential to turn new ideas into market opportunities and job growth would unleash new sources of economic energy among the former Soviet states. The resulting success stories may help dispel the fear and cynicism currently associated with business startups in the region.

The governments in post–Soviet countries have much work to do to combat bribery and other forms of endemic corruption and to change the perception that they are risky environments for business startups.

08

Middle East/ North Africa

Algeria, Bahrain, Egypt, Iran, Iraq, Israel, Jordan, Kuwait, Lebanon, Libya, Morocco, Palestinian Territories, Qatar, Saudi Arabia, Syria, Tunisia, Turkey, United Arab Emirates, Yemen

14%

of employees in the Middle East/North Africa are engaged.

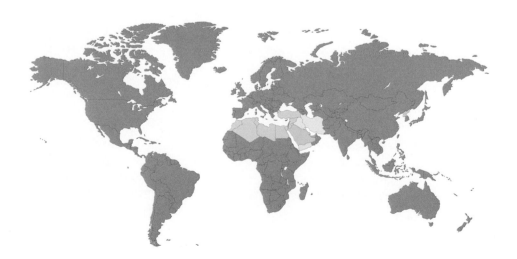

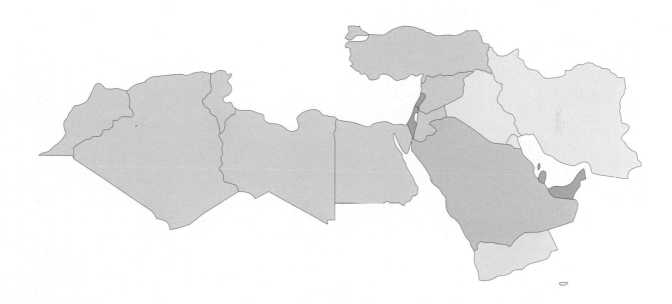

% Employed full time
for an employer

8%   72%
Yemen   UAE

See the appendix for "good jobs" data, by country.

58%

of MENA residents say they would rather have a job working for the government than for a business.

VS.

37%

globally

THE MIDDLE EAST/NORTH AFRICA (MENA) region includes countries with very different levels of economic development and labor market conditions, from the gleaming towers of oil-rich Gulf Cooperation Council countries like Qatar and the United Arab Emirates to the desperate poverty and chronic instability of Yemen and Libya. As a whole, economic growth in the region is stagnating partly as a result of low oil prices and the fallout from brutal ongoing conflicts in Syria, Iraq and Yemen.

Historically among Arab countries, the government has been citizens' primary employer, and this remains the case in much of the region. Recently, however, falling oil prices and alarmingly high levels of youth unemployment have led even the region's wealthiest governments to make private-sector job growth a priority.

Lack of private-sector investment, often coupled with a mismatch between citizens' skills and training and the needs of private employers, lead many in the region to seek government jobs. Gallup finds that 58% of MENA residents overall say they would rather have a job working for the government than for a business, while 27% say the opposite. Within MENA, Egyptians are the most likely, at 69%, to say they would prefer a government job, while just 16% say they would rather work for a business. By contrast, in economically developed regions such as the U.S./Canada, Western Europe and Australia/New Zealand, most residents prefer private-sector employment over government jobs.

> *Lack of private-sector investment, often coupled with a mismatch between citizens' skills and training and the needs of private employers, lead many in the region to seek government jobs.*

MAJORITY OF MENA RESIDENTS PREFER WORKING FOR GOVERNMENT OVER BUSINESS

Would you rather have a job working for the government or working for a business?

Country	Government %	Business %
Egypt	69	16
Qatar	67	27
Turkey	64	29
Saudi Arabia	63	28
Jordan	62	29
United Arab Emirates	62	32
Yemen	62	15
Kuwait	61	31
Bahrain	60	33
Algeria	59	19
Iran	51	41
Libya	51	41
Morocco	51	20
Iraq	48	35
Palestinian Territories	46	33
Tunisia	46	26
Lebanon	42	25
Israel	37	37
Syria	33	36

Several factors limit human capital development in the region. Among the most prevalent are religious and cultural norms that restrict women's participation in the labor force. Seventy percent of the region's women aged 23 to 65 are out of the workforce (i.e., not employed and not looking for a job). These constraints limit the total proportion of working-age adults who have a job. Overall, 45% of MENA residents aged 23 to 65 are out of the workforce — the highest regional figure in the world.

However, rising education levels among women and changing attitudes toward women's rights among the region's young people suggest the region is poised for growth in female labor force participation. While conditions vary by country, one hurdle is that educational opportunities for women have generally been quicker to expand in Arab societies than have job opportunities. The result is that just 30% of women in the MENA region with four or more years of higher education work full time for employers, versus 50% of highly educated men. Expanding private-sector job opportunities give a higher proportion of educated women avenues to contribute meaningfully to their country's economy.

> *Rising education levels among women and changing attitudes toward women's rights among the region's young people suggest the region is poised for growth in female labor force participation.*

The economic diversification that Arab countries need will require sustained efforts by both government and business leaders. Job No. 1 will be to support the development of small- and medium-sized enterprises in the private sector. The region will need to improve access to financing and reform education systems so that growing businesses have access to appropriately trained workers.

For their part, private-sector employers in the region can appeal to young people by emphasizing a strong sense of purpose in their organization, as well as a focus on ongoing developmental opportunities for employees. Like millennial-age residents in other regions, many young Arabs are idealistic and future-oriented. Private businesses that offer them chances to bring about positive change in the region and to continually develop their own potential may be particularly likely to overcome the regional bias toward government jobs.

MENA SPOTLIGHT: UNITED ARAB EMIRATES

Focusing on managerial talent could help the UAE boost positivity among public employees.

In less than two decades, the United Arab Emirates (UAE) has emerged as one of the Middle East's most vibrant economic hubs. The country's two largest cities, Dubai and Abu Dhabi, have rocketed to global prominence as destinations for business and tourism, with breathtaking skyscrapers, ultramodern transportation and IT infrastructure, lavish shopping mega-centers, and stunning beaches.

The nation's dramatic success story would not have been possible if the UAE wasn't a model of political and social stability in a region where development in many countries is hindered by conflict. Vice President and Prime Minister of the United Arab Emirates and Ruler of Dubai, His Highness Sheikh Mohammed bin Rashid, recently declared, "Happiness and positivity in the UAE are a lifestyle, a government commitment and a spirit uniting the UAE community."

However, the government does not take that stability for granted — it has recently embarked on a number of national initiatives intended to better understand and promote happiness among UAE residents.

> *"Happiness and positivity in the UAE are a lifestyle, a government commitment and a spirit uniting the UAE community."*
> *— Vice President and Prime Minister of the United Arab Emirates and Ruler of Dubai, His Highness Sheikh Mohammed bin Rashid*

The public sector still accounts for approximately 90% of jobs held by Emirati nationals, so understanding how workplace conditions affect employees' emotional health and life satisfaction is a priority in the government's happiness research. Accordingly, Gallup worked in the UAE on a broader workplace model designed to achieve this understanding and guide improving employee happiness initiatives.

Model Links Life Satisfaction to Engagement, Trust and Positivity at Work

Gallup's initial phase of research has guided the development of a theoretical model consisting of four components, including engagement, that help explain the link between employees' feelings about their job and their overall life satisfaction:

1. **engagement:** the sense of emotional attachment to one's work that supports high levels of motivation and productivity

2. **trust:** feelings of security and confidence in one's leadership, managers and coworkers that help employees feel good about their relationships at work, and the idea that they are valued members of a cohesive team

3. **positivity:** a sense of optimism based on employees' identification with the mission of their organization, as well as their opportunity to focus on and develop their strengths

4. **integration:** a wider role of the workplace toward employee well-being, work-life balance and community involvement

Employees who have positive perceptions in each of these areas, according to the theory, are more likely to see their work as a calling rather than just a job, and the resulting sense of purpose makes them more optimistic about their lives overall.

Talented Managers Are Essential to Workplace Happiness

Workgroup-level managers are in a position to have a powerful impact on each of these components. Gallup research shows that managers are responsible for at least 70% of the variance in their employees' engagement. Yet, even with so much riding on this, managers are often promoted due to their previous success in a nonmanagerial role or simply due to having experience in the particular organization, agency or field of expertise. Instead, organizations should select managers based on their inherent talent for managing — including their ability to foster positive relationships with their team members while keeping them motivated and focused on outcomes that are both meaningful and attainable.

Further, Gallup encourages clients with rapidly rising proportions of younger employees, as many employers in the MENA region have, to radically alter their performance management processes in step with changing expectations. Annual performance reviews conducted in many organizations should give way to constant, continual and customized feedback that reinforces positive behavior and provides guidance and support when performance does not meet expectations.

Talented managers focus on linking employees' roles to their organization's or agency's wider purpose, with the manager acting as a coach for employees, coaxing the best possible performance out of them and helping them fully maximize their potential. When employees feel they are at their best and are authentically recognized as such (or understand clearly where they need support), they have little doubt that they are making a positive contribution. The resulting sense of fulfillment may be the most important factor for ensuring that the quality of employees' working lives contributes to their overall happiness.

70%

Gallup research shows that managers are responsible for at least 70% of the variance in their employees' engagement.

Talented managers focus on linking employees' roles to their organization's or agency's wider purpose, with the manager acting as a coach for employees, coaxing the best possible performance out of them and helping them fully maximize their potential.

09

Sub-Saharan Africa

Angola, Benin, Botswana, Burkina Faso, Burundi, Cameroon, Central African Republic, Chad, Congo (Kinshasa), Congo (Brazzaville), Ethiopia, Gabon, Ghana, Guinea, Ivory Coast, Kenya, Lesotho, Liberia, Madagascar, Malawi, Mali, Mauritania, Mauritius, Mozambique, Namibia, Niger, Nigeria, Rwanda, Senegal, Sierra Leone, Somalia, South Africa, South Sudan, Sudan, Tanzania, Togo, Uganda, Zambia, Zimbabwe

17%

of employees in sub-Saharan Africa are engaged.

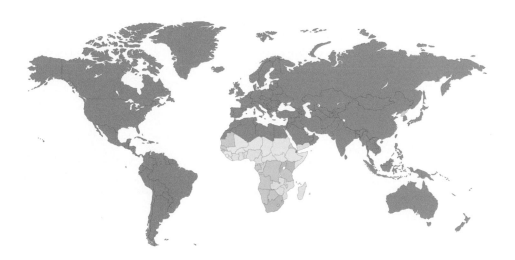

122

% Employed full time
for an employer

5%   42%
Niger   Mauritius

See the appendix for "good jobs" data, by country.

14%

*of working–age adults in
sub-Saharan Africa are employed
full time for an employer.*

vs.

32%

globally

SUB-SAHARAN AFRICA REMAINS THE WORLD'S least economically developed region, with a shortage of formal job opportunities and inadequate supports for business growth and human capital development. Overall, just 14% of adults aged 23 to 65 are employed full time for an employer — Gallup's definition of a good job. This is the lowest regional figure worldwide. Even among the relatively small proportion of residents in sub-Saharan Africa who have four or more years of higher education, just 34% say they work full time for an employer — an indicator that the region's labor markets are failing to direct human resources to where they are needed most.

With the end of the global commodity boom that lifted many African economies in the 2000s, growth in the region has fallen to its weakest pace in two decades. Thirty percent of sub-Saharan Africans aged 23 to 65 describe themselves as self-employed — typically they are engaged in subsistence activities (e.g., small-scale farming or street vending) with little potential for growth under current conditions. Just 25% of residents who say they own a business also say they have formally registered their business — also the lowest regional percentage in the world.

Sub–Saharan Africa remains the world's least economically developed region, with a shortage of formal job opportunities and inadequate supports for business growth and human capital development.

Solutions for promoting development and formal-sector job growth in sub-Saharan Africa have been hard to come by. Poor infrastructure, corruption and weak rule of law are among the barriers to private investment in the region. The danger of relying too heavily on commodity exports has become clear, further highlighting the need for human capital development and economic diversification. Lack of formal employment is relatively consistent throughout the region. Of the 39 countries Gallup surveyed in sub-Saharan Africa, the only ones in which more than about one in four working-age residents are employed full time for an employer are Mauritius at 42% and South Africa at 27%.

25%

of residents who say they own a business also say they have formally registered their business.

Of the 39 countries Gallup surveyed in sub-Saharan Africa, the only ones in which more than about one in four working-age residents are employed full time for an employer are:

42%

Mauritius

AND

27%

South Africa

MISMATCHED SKILLS LEAD TO WIDESPREAD JOBLESSNESS IN MORE-DEVELOPED AFRICAN ECONOMIES

The countries in sub-Saharan Africa that have made notable progress toward social stability and economic diversification in recent decades now face an urgent need to equip more residents with the necessary skills and knowledge for maintaining that progress. In South Africa and Botswana, for example, residents are less likely to be self-employed at subsistence level, but both countries face massive unemployment; currently, 20% of residents aged 23 to 65 in each say they are not employed and are looking for work.

South Africa, in particular, has been regarded as one of the region's most promising emerging markets, but in recent years, the country's GDP growth has virtually ground to a halt. One conclusion from the World Economic Forum on Africa in 2016 was that education and training for future skills are critical to helping the country's large youth population meet the challenges posed by the fast-paced technological and demographic changes the country will face in the coming years.

Targeted, high-quality education is among the most critical factors in empowering more Africans to contribute to economic progress in their country. Given limited resources, however, governments must seek approaches that maximize the benefit of every hour that students spend in educational pursuits.

> *The countries in sub-Saharan Africa that have made notable progress toward social stability and economic diversification in recent decades now face an urgent need to equip more residents with the necessary skills and knowledge for maintaining that progress.*

Gallup's education research points to two strategies that are likely to help:

- Incentivizing local businesses to partner with colleges and universities to provide experiences that help students put their learning to practical use. In 2015, Gallup conducted a survey of 1,550 education experts from 149 countries in conjunction with the World Innovation Summit for Education (WISE); the strongest consensus was on the need for more collaboration between schools and employers — for example, in co-op programs, internships and mentoring arrangements.

- Making self-discovery and strengths development key curricular goals so that students can identify areas in which they are most interested and in which they are most likely to create economic energy. Viewing their future through the lens of the potential contribution their strengths would allow them to make would offer a sense of hope that may be absent otherwise.

20%

of residents aged 23 to 65 in South Africa and Botswana say they are not employed and are looking for work.

Accelerating the pace of human capital development is crucial to promoting growth in African countries that is both sustainable and broad-based. It's hardly a simple proposition. But the tools they need to make it happen are becoming more readily accessible every day, as low-cost forms of information and communication technology help broaden access to critical supports like education, healthcare and banking services, and new strategies help individuals turn their inherent strengths into the practical skills they need to thrive.

Accelerating the pace of human capital development is crucial to promoting growth in African countries that is both sustainable and broad-based.

10

East Asia

China, Hong Kong, Japan, Mongolia, South Korea, Taiwan

6%

of employees in East Asia are engaged.

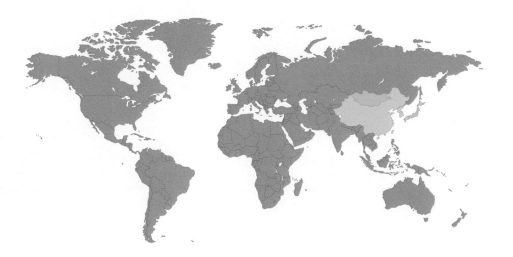

% Employed full time
for an employer

32%	51%
China	Taiwan

See the appendix for "good jobs" data, by country.

94%

of employees in East Asia are not engaged or are actively disengaged.

vs.

85%

globally

MOST EAST ASIAN COUNTRIES HAVE extremely low proportions of employees who are engaged at work, even relative to the startlingly small global engagement figure of 15%. The corresponding population-level percentages do not reach double-digits in Japan (6%), South Korea (7%), China (6%), Hong Kong (5%) or Taiwan (7%). The consistency in these results suggests that cultural norms influence employee engagement throughout the region.

Among the most pervasive of the cultural norms in East Asia is a collectivist mindset that individual needs and desires concede to organizational goals. In Japan and South Korea, this mindset has bred a culture of overwork that is, in many cases, proving harmful to employees' health and well-being; this tendency has recently raised concerns in China as well.

Cultivating employee engagement requires management strategies that address the needs and contributions of individual employees — helping employees remain highly productive and bonded to their organization while vastly improving the quality of their day-to-day life. Workplaces that focus on employee engagement optimize employees' contributions and make them enthusiastic about their job. Helping employees maximize the quality of their time spent working may also help remove some of the pressure to work long hours and therefore encourage a healthier work-life balance.

> *Workplaces that focus on employee engagement optimize employees' contributions and make them enthusiastic about their job.*

Globally, employed residents in East Asia are among the least likely to strongly agree that they like what they do each day — at 17%.

Among employees who are engaged at work, however, that figure skyrockets: 57% of *engaged* employees in the region strongly agree that they like what they do each day, compared with 16% of those who are not engaged and 10% of those who are actively disengaged.

Globally, employed residents in East Asia are among the least likely to strongly agree that they like what they do each day — at 17%.

EAST ASIAN ENGAGED EMPLOYEES MUCH MORE LIKELY TO AGREE THEY LIKE WHAT THEY DO

% Strongly agree with "I like what I do each day"

■ Engaged ■ Not engaged ■ Actively disengaged

57

16

10

EAST ASIA SPOTLIGHT: CHINA

In China, new money and new buying habits require a new understanding of the link between employee and customer engagement.

Decades of economic growth in China helped today's workers earn almost three times more than they did 10 years ago. The result is a lot of new money.

By 2020, the middle class in China is expected to number almost 400 million consumers, whose shopping accounts for 65% of China's GDP. Not coincidentally, household income is at least $5 trillion a year, discretionary spending is up and 77% of residents tell Gallup their standard of living is getting better.

China's new money is creating new buying habits. These days, quality matters as much or more than price — especially among those in the millennial generation, who are now in their 20s and early 30s. Consumers are not afraid to pay for experiences, and the service industry is booming. For the first time ever, China's service sector accounts for more than half of the country's GDP. And Chinese customers, like customers everywhere, are more loyal and lucrative when they're emotionally engaged in their purchasing experience — Gallup calls that customer engagement. But, China's economy has long been predicated on producing large quantities of goods quickly, mostly for purchase in other countries. The need to engage Chinese consumers is relatively new to most companies.

The changes in consumerism in China have created a problem for China's business leaders. On one side of the economy is a very advanced manufacturing industry, and on the other is a burgeoning customer base. In the middle is a gap where customer engagement should be. It seems like a big gap to fill, but it is not. It's an *enormous* gap.

Filling it is going to take an equally enormous change. And it has to start with leadership.

Engaging a New Customer Base Starts on the Front Lines

Business leadership in China is hierarchical, as it is in most Asian countries. The power imbalance works its way down to team leads, who often have tremendous power over every aspect of the job, including promotions and pay. That kind of top-down leadership can hobble employee engagement. Tellingly, China's engagement rate is only 6% — globally, 15% of workers are engaged, and in the U.S., it's 33%.

Engagement is relevant because engaged workers spur engaged customers, and engaged customers spur profit. Gallup data from a variety of industries and target audiences shows that engaged customers represent a 23% premium in terms of share of wallet, profitability, revenue and relationship growth compared with the average customer; actively disengaged customers represent a 13% discount in those same measures.

6%

of China's workers are engaged.

To engage its service sector, China needs to engage its workers. Forward-thinking leaders are already seeing the benefits in doing just that, but some are misplacing their efforts. Leadership development programs tend to focus on the upper and middle ranks. Very little money and time are dedicated to the lowest echelons of management — and even less are available to front-line workers.

Furthermore, when business leaders do turn their attention to engaging front-line employees, they may focus predominantly on strategies geared toward younger workers. Like members of their age cohort globally, the Chinese millennial generation is big and has a reputation for being startlingly different than previous generations. Indeed, Gallup has found that millennials are more prone to require a mission and purpose in their work, as well as more coaching and development than their older counterparts in the workplace. Delivering on those principles is important, especially when shoring up engagement among service-sector employees.

However, companies should also take care to respect the values of older employees who often don't feel they need as much attention as younger workers seem to — and may be offended by the suggestion that they do. They grew up and entered the workforce in a very different culture, one that placed far more emphasis on deference to authority. Thus, a flurry of management attention to the needs of millennials may leave their elders feeling their contributions aren't being appropriately respected. It's an example of the kind of delicate challenge that requires managers to understand employees' differing perspectives and develop flexible strategies for engaging each one accordingly.

Engaged Employees Could Help Their Service-Sector Employers Reap Massive Gains

To get the most out of its service sector, Chinese leadership needs to shift its focus to the diverse needs of its labor force. The foundation for creating an engaged workforce is already in place: Human resources departments have more muscle than they did even five years ago, young workers expect and get individual attention, and the corporate community understands that GDP growth requires expanding their notions of how things are done. Those factors are all fundamental to implementing employee engagement initiatives. Now it's time to build on that foundation by measuring and improving employee and customer engagement.

If Chinese business leaders come to a better understanding of employee engagement, they will be far better positioned to develop front-line strategies for improving customer engagement too. Doing so would require a new leadership approach in an old culture, which isn't easily executed in Asia. Still, the incentive is clear: the staggering amount of money to be made from 400 million engaged customers spending 23% more in a service-sector economy.

EAST ASIA SPOTLIGHT: JAPAN

Japanese firms are past due for a realignment of people management.

In the 1980s, many believed that Japan was on the brink of global economic domination. Automobile manufacturers Honda, Toyota and Nissan and consumer electronics firms like Sony, Panasonic and Toshiba were becoming household names everywhere, and the country's economy had become the second largest in the world.

Then, in the early 1990s, the country's turbocharged rise came to a sputtering halt with the bursting of a huge asset price bubble and the ensuing "lost decade" of economic decline. Today, the Japanese remain more likely to say the country's economy is getting worse (48%) than to say it is getting better (32%).

Today in Japan:

48%

vs.

32%

believe the country's economy is getting worse.

believe the country's economy is getting better.

Many factors have contributed to Japan's current fiscal malaise. Massive stimulus plans have saddled the government with an unprecedented debt burden. The country's rapidly aging population is shrinking the pool of working-age citizens, even as its anti-immigration bias limits the entry of foreign workers to supplement its labor force. Most recently, U.S. President Donald Trump blocked progress toward a regional trade deal (the Trans-Pacific Partnership) that may have given Japanese exports a boost.

However, it has become increasingly evident that there is another problem embedded in the Japanese workforce — one that may be just as detrimental to the country's economic future as its structural and demographic challenges. Ironically, it's a result of the postwar arrangement Japanese workers and their employers made that fueled the country's 20th-century rise: "lifetime employment" in return for unwavering loyalty to the organization.

Money was scarce after World War II, so Japanese businesses and governments offered workers security in lieu of hefty salaries. At the time, it was a useful arrangement. But now, it encourages employees to overlook or cover up the effects of poor leadership or mismanagement, resulting in problems ballooning into full-fledged crises. In recent years, prominent Japanese companies have suffered scandals resulting from falsified or hidden defects in automotive designs, fuel economy systems and balance sheets — all due to misguided loyalty.

An overwhelming sense of duty has led to a culture of overwork that has many employees putting in dangerously long hours. The result, according to the government's 2016 white paper on the topic, is increased rates of serious physical and mental health problems — even suicide. The problem is so pervasive that "death by overwork" is a medically recognized cause of fatality.

Employee Improvement Priorities

In 2015, just 35% of Japanese employees agreed with the statement, "In the last seven days, I have felt active and productive every day," by giving a "4" or "5" response on a five-point agreement scale. By comparison, 73% of employees in the U.S. rated their agreement at "4" or "5," as did 65% of German employees. What's more, Japanese employees under age 50 are less likely than those 50 and older to agree — 29% vs. 43%, respectively.

Younger Japanese employees, in particular, are increasingly questioning the premise implied by the country's intense work culture: that being present is the same as being productive. Lifelong employment is no longer offered at most companies, and Prime Minister Shinzo Abe's government is actively working with employers to reduce the perceived pressure to work long hours.

One way to reduce pressure is to convince employees that over the long term, they can best contribute to their company by assigning top priority to their well-being. Gallup researchers have found that workers who score highly on five elements of personal well-being — physical, financial, social, community and purpose — miss fewer workdays, are more productive, are healthier and adapt to change more quickly.

The Japanese government has not failed to recognize the business case for placing more focus on workers' well-being. "Work style reform is not only a social issue, but also an economic one," Abe has said. Abe is proposing an updated economic bargain — different in detail, but identical in purpose — between business and labor.

But in the middle of business and labor is the manager. Workers will believe that their well-being is important only if managers make it important, and although Japanese businesses are rightfully renowned for their training programs, that training does not typically include people management.

An important benefit of good people management is higher employee engagement, which boosts productivity, innovation, profitability, safety and a host of other lucrative outcomes. Japan's 6% engagement rate is dismal, and its economy has stagnated for years. That should be reason enough for business leaders to double down on engagement — but engagement also promotes factors that employees need to lead healthy lives in general.

Slow economic development, inflexibility and a shrinking labor pool are all urgent issues, and implementing a focus on well-being, strengths-based development and engagement can go a long way toward a remedy. If Japanese business leaders can reconnect with the spirit of reinvention that led to the country's remarkable rise after World War II, Japan could amaze the world once again.

THE TALENT FACTOR
Japanese companies can energize their workforces by focusing on employees' strengths.

The changes needed to put Japanese businesses and employees on a more sustainable path to success may seem daunting, but they need not be overly complicated. There are certain fundamental principles that promote engagement and productivity in all types of workplaces. None is more important than applying a strengths-based approach to hiring and developing employees.

In Japanese companies, strategies for assessing and maximizing employees' strengths offer the potential for providing a badly needed jolt of energy. The kigyo shudan system of enterprise groups that Japan adopted in the 1950s provided security and helped companies plan for long-term growth, but it also produced hierarchies that became slow to make decisions and adapt to changing circumstances. By contrast, strengths-based companies fit job roles to employees' strengths, resulting in higher individual productivity. Allowing employees to focus on their strengths helps companies overcome barriers to opportunity — whether they are based on gender, age or any other outdated criteria — to maximize productivity in any given role.

Adding strengths-based development to corporate cultures should also help rectify the notion that more hours equates to more productivity. A 2015 Gallup analysis finds that employees who agree that they use their strengths every day are six times more likely to be engaged at work, 8% more productive and 15% less likely to quit their job than those who do not agree that they use their strengths at work. Strengths-based cultures make companies stronger because they tend to promote intellectual diversity among decision-makers — for example, by diminishing the barriers to women becoming leaders.

A 2015 Gallup analysis finds that employees who agree
that they use their strengths every day are:

6x
more likely to be
engaged at work

8%
more
productive

15%
less likely to quit
their job

than those who do not agree that they use their
strengths at work.

The shift to strengths-based practices may not be easy at first — indeed, any significant change to traditional Japanese management practices is bound to meet some resistance. But the idea of embracing and building on one's strengths is universal; in Japan, nearly 500,000 individuals have already taken the CliftonStrengths assessment. The growing strengths movement is promising news for Japanese workers because it highlights the notion that working smarter can be just as beneficial to organizations as working harder — and more likely to help employees strike a healthy work-life balance.

JAPAN'S WORKING WOMEN

Japanese leaders must change the country's way of working to help women participate more fully in the country's labor force.

One facet of Japan's business culture that keeps it from moving forward is its male-dominated composition. Working women tend to be an undervalued resource, particularly when it comes to their management skills. Just 11% of Japanese managers are women — in the United States, women hold 39% of management positions.

A recent global study by Gallup and the International Labor Organization (ILO) sheds light on the dilemma Japan's working women face. When asked, "Would you prefer to work at a paid job or stay at home and take care of your family and the housework, or would you prefer to do both?" 56% of Japanese women say they would prefer to do both. Among younger Japanese women — those aged 15 to 29 — that figure rises to 64%. Despite the workforce's cultural predisposition toward long hours, most Japanese women do not want to choose between having a family and having a career.

The result is a Catch-22: Women's traditional role as mother and homemaker makes many unable to compete with men in a business environment that demands that workers prioritize their employer. This relative disadvantage represents an insurmountable barrier to advancement in companies where promotion to leadership positions is based on tenure or the capacity to work longer and harder than one's colleagues. When asked what their biggest work-related challenge is, Japan's working women are far more likely to say family (58%) than the demands of the job (15%) or even just getting a job (2%).

In turn, women's inability to achieve higher-paying positions helps preserve the traditional status of men as the family's primary breadwinner. The Gallup-ILO study finds that just 11% of employed women in Japan say their job is the main source of their household's income, and only 22% say it is even a significant source. By contrast, almost half of working men (47%) say their job is the main source of their household's income, and an additional 34% say it is a significant source.

Women's traditional role as mother and homemaker makes many unable to compete with men in a business environment that demands that workers prioritize their employer.

The Gallup-ILO study finds that:

11%

AND

of employed women in Japan
say their job is the main source
of their household's income

22%

say their job is a
significant source of their
household's income

Japan's leaders understand the need to change the country's way of working. Among the structural components of Abe's economic reform program — popularly known as "Abenomics" — is a set of labor laws intended to increase the number of women in the workforce. Abe has promised 400,000 openings in day cares by 2018, shorter work hours and a focus on increasing women's presence in management. Abenomics originally called for moving women into 30% of management positions by 2020, but that percentage has since been revised to 15%. "The female labor force in Japan is the most underutilized resource," Abe told the World Economic Forum in 2014.

Addressing the problem means no longer discounting the vast amount of leadership and management talent that Japanese women represent. It's the kind of talent that may be particularly beneficial to Japanese organizations: A recent analysis of results from millions of individuals who have completed Gallup's CliftonStrengths assessment finds that women tend to rank higher than men on relationship-building themes. Those are exactly the talents that companies need if they are to refocus their management systems to include an emphasis on people rather than on processes alone.

An important benefit of good people management is higher employee engagement, which boosts productivity, innovation, profitability, safety and a host of other lucrative outcomes.

11

Southeast Asia

Cambodia, Indonesia, Malaysia, Myanmar, Philippines, Singapore, Thailand, Vietnam

19%
of employees in Southeast Asia are engaged.

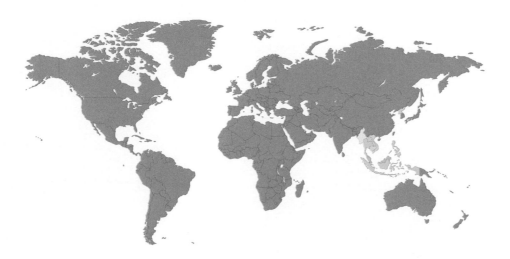

% Employed full time
for an employer

16%
Cambodia

60%
Singapore

See the appendix for "good jobs" data, by country.

22%

of working–age adults in
Southeast Asia are employed full
time for an employer.

VS.

32%

globally

IN RECENT YEARS, SOUTHEAST ASIA has been one of the world's most economically dynamic regions. Rapid economic expansion among members of the Association of Southeast Asian Nations (ASEAN) has led some analysts to regard the regional bloc as a global growth engine, at least for the short term. However, as a recent United Nations Educational, Scientific and Cultural Organization (UNESCO) report noted, rapid growth has brought widening disparities in living standards and economic opportunities to Southeast Asia, as some residents are better-positioned than others to take advantage of new technology and infrastructure improvements.

The close relationship between residents' education level and employment status reflects the disparities. Informal employment is common; just 39% of business owners in the region tell Gallup they have formally registered their business, with many of the remainder involved in subsistence activities such as small-scale farming. Regionally, just 22% of residents say they are employed full time for an employer — Gallup's definition of a good job. However, this figure rises to 42% among those with at least four years of higher education.

Rapid growth has brought widening disparities in living standards and economic opportunities to Southeast Asia, as some residents are better-positioned than others to take advantage of new technology and infrastructure improvements.

These findings underscore the critical importance of widespread access to a high-quality education in Southeast Asia to help the region's large youth populations navigate and benefit from the rapid changes taking place in their countries. Thus, it's a positive sign that the region is also marked by unusually high levels of confidence in local schools. More than three-fourths of residents in Thailand (88%), Singapore (87%), the Philippines (83%), Vietnam (82%), Myanmar (77%) and Malaysia (76%) say they are satisfied with the education system in the city or area where they live.

SOUTHEAST ASIA SPOTLIGHT: SINGAPORE

A focus on employee development may give Singaporean firms an edge in the region's war for talent.

In an economically thriving Southeast Asian region, Singapore is the beating heart — a financial, high-tech and transportation hub with 2% unemployment and a per capita GDP higher than that of most developed nations. Sixty percent of Singaporeans aged 23 to 65 work full time for an employer — one of the highest rates worldwide — and 87% of Singaporean adults say they are satisfied with their standard of living — easily the highest percentage in Southeast Asia.

Moreover, Singapore's businesses appear to be improving workplace conditions that enable the country's employees to be fully engaged and productive. Gallup surveys between 2014 and 2016 find that 23% of employees are engaged at work — a substantial rise from just 9% found in surveys conducted in 2011 and 2012.

87%

of Singaporean adults say they are satisfied with their standard of living.

Singaporean employees' level of engagement has risen in recent years.

9%   vs.   23%

engaged in 2011-2012

engaged in 2014-2016

From conversations with human resources leaders in Singapore, Gallup has noted a shift in workforce development strategies — including a movement away from tenure-based progression to performance-based development. Such a change could certainly account for rising engagement among the city-state's employees because it implies that workgroup managers are more effectively supporting them for maximum productivity. For example, employed Singaporeans are now significantly more likely than they were in 2012 to strongly agree that they have opportunities to do what they do best at work and that there is someone at work who encourages their development.

Singapore's business leaders now have an opportunity to build on these management gains to make the city-state home to one of the world's most highly engaged workforces. Doing so, however, will require an ongoing focus on elements of workplace culture that help employees find psychological gratification in their work.

> *Singapore's business leaders now have an opportunity to build on these management gains to make the city-state home to one of the world's most highly engaged workforces.*

Personal Growth Is the Key to High Productivity and Profitability

One aspect of Singapore's culture that may pose a challenge in terms of employees' sense of personal fulfillment is the tendency to focus on group outcomes and achievements, largely to the exclusion of individual accomplishments. While team outcomes are a very important area of focus, Gallup's research shows that managers can heighten team members' psychological investment in their work through ongoing coaching relationships that focus on employees' individual goals. Each worker has distinctive strengths and likely somewhat different career goals.

The best managers in the world focus on the unique strengths and aspirations of each person they manage. They achieve this kind of individualization by increasing the frequency of casual conversations that they have with their employees about personal growth and career development. The result is that employees feel more empowered and engaged and are less likely to seek other job opportunities. Retention is an important concern given that, according to a 2015 Randstad Workmonitor report, 67% of Singaporeans believe they can find a new job within six months.

While high performance is the optimum goal for government and business leaders in Singapore, a culture of personal growth is what resonates most with employees — and managers are in the unique position to promote the development of every employee. Culturally, managers are regarded highly. They can take advantage of the esteem that their position affords them to connect with employees regularly as they foster such mentor-coach relationships.

With Southeast Asian cities competing for talent and business, including two of Singapore's closest neighbors, Bangkok and Jakarta, it will be the businesses that support and nurture their human capital that will ultimately win the competitive race to attract and retain a talented workforce. Business leadership that supports employees' personal relationships with managers who care about their development will make the difference.

The best managers in the world focus on the unique strengths and aspirations of each person they manage.

12

South Asia

Afghanistan, Bangladesh, Bhutan, India, Nepal, Pakistan, Sri Lanka

14%

of employees in South Asia are engaged.

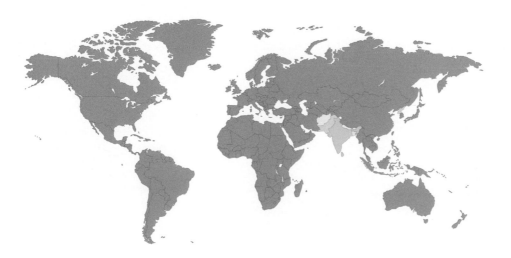

% Employed full time
for an employer

11%   31%
Afghanistan   India

See the appendix for "good jobs" data, by country.

28%

of working–age adults in South Asia are employed full time for an employer.

vs.

32%

globally

DESPITE PROGRESS TOWARD POVERTY REDUCTION in much of the region as a whole, South Asia is still characterized by low levels of development and economies dominated by informal sectors. Just 37% of business owners in the region tell Gallup they have formally registered their business; many toil at family enterprises at subsistence level, with little or no potential for job creation. Overall, 28% of South Asian residents aged 23 to 65 say they are employed full time for an employer — Gallup's definition of a good job. Only in sub-Saharan Africa, Southeast Asia and the Middle East/North Africa (MENA) region is this figure lower.

As in the MENA region, economic productivity in South Asia is limited by cultural and religious norms that restrict women's workforce participation. Two-thirds of the region's women aged 23 to 65 (66%) are out of the workforce (i.e., not employed and not looking for a job), while just 14% are employed full time for an employer. The opportunity cost in terms of human capital is particularly high when it comes to well-educated women. Regionally, 48% of women aged 23 to 65 who have four or more years of education beyond high school are out of the workforce versus 21% of men with this level of education.

Economic productivity in South Asia is limited by cultural and religious norms that restrict women's workforce participation.

66% of the region's women aged 23 to 65 are out of the workforce.

vs.

14% of the region's women aged 23 to 65 are employed full time for an employer.

MANY OF SOUTH ASIA'S BEST-EDUCATED WOMEN ARE NOT
WORKFORCE PARTICIPANTS

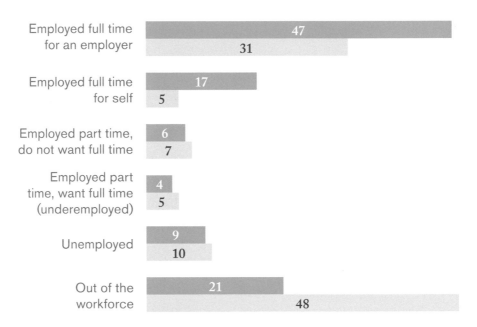

■ % Men with higher education ■ % Women with higher education

Employed full time for an employer: 47 / 31
Employed full time for self: 17 / 5
Employed part time, do not want full time: 6 / 7
Employed part time, want full time (underemployed): 4 / 5
Unemployed: 9 / 10
Out of the workforce: 21 / 48

In India, which accounts for the vast majority of the region's population, Prime Minister Narendra Modi was elected in 2014 on the promise that he would make pro-market reforms and spur private-sector job growth. Three years later, his government appears to be delivering on that promise: The Indian economy is expected to grow at more than 7% through the 2019 and 2020 fiscal years, due largely to private investment.

The Indian economy is expected to grow at more than 7% through the 2019 and 2020 fiscal years, due largely to private investment.

Solid growth has been forecasted despite the government's drastic decision under Modi in November 2016 to demonetize the economy in an attempt to make illicit transactions more difficult and remove counterfeit notes from circulation. Demonetization resulted in short-term havoc, particularly in poorer regions where most residents had little access to banking infrastructure. But in the ensuing months, it spurred millions of previously "unbanked" Indians to get bank accounts and led to the rapid spread of digital payment systems. As the World Bank has emphasized in its development with Gallup of a global financial inclusion index (FINDEX), access to financial services gives people opportunities to save, invest and contribute to economic progress in their country.

India's economic growth has been predominantly in the country's rapidly developing urban areas, where many residents work for large companies like the Tata Group, headquartered in Mumbai. But currently, just 13% of employed Indians are engaged at work. India's predominant employers have the potential to improve productivity and well-being in their country — improvements that would help build on the government's efforts to establish a more business-friendly environment and help sustain the country's economic momentum. Employers' first step should be focusing on the elements that contribute to employees' motivation and enthusiasm.

13%
of employed Indians are engaged at work.

SOUTH ASIA SPOTLIGHT: INDIA

Dismal engagement levels among Indian workers hurt productivity, which the country desperately needs to improve.

One can rarely go wrong describing India as "more so" — more people, more languages, more economic growth, more companies, more noise. And the same goes for business problems.

The Indian economy has been booming in recent years, but with rapid growth comes rapid change. On top of the structural changes that come with technological innovation, in 2016, the Indian government instituted a radical change in the way business is done by demonetizing the economy in favor of digital transactions.

India's businesses will have to be nimble to manage all this change and keep the country's economy on track. But many still maintain a rigid, hierarchical leadership structure that's not built for speed. This structure not only hurts market response, but it's an obstacle to productivity. Productivity gains are important everywhere in the world, of course, but in India, more so.

Nudging the work culture out of its hierarchical construct won't be easy — it is a culture built on generations of patriarchal leadership structures. Family-owned businesses account for almost two-thirds of India's GDP and about half of its workforce.

This traditional way of structuring businesses not only makes Indian companies less adaptable — in many cases, it also affects the way employees do their job. Hierarchical boss-employee relationships stifle innovation and productivity and discourage employee engagement. They reward obedience more than outcome — "looking busy" more than actually being productive.

Command-and-Control Workplaces Curb Employee Engagement and Productivity

Engagement depends on the fulfillment of essential workplace conditions that empower employees. When organizations meet those needs, workers are more inclined to make the kinds of emotional, company-centric decisions — whether to use a machine carefully, whether to help a coworker — that boost productivity. Command-and-control management does little to create engagement because it is essentially impersonal. This management style is in businesses across the world — but especially in India.

For most working Indians, the demands of management and engagement are blended with the complications of family relationships, especially in higher leadership. And the one-on-one coaching and emotional involvement necessary for employee engagement is not part of the typical business culture.

Millennial Workers Seek Jobs That Give Them a Sense of Purpose

India's management style norms may present a particular problem for millennial workers, who are forecasted to account for 64% of all Indian workers by 2021. Millennials are more likely than any other age group to require coaching and development, need a sense of purpose from their work, and desire ongoing conversations with their manager. That's the foundation of an engaging manager-employee relationship, but Gallup finds that Indian millennials aren't feeling it: 13% of employed Indians born between 1980 and 1996 are engaged at work, similar to the 14% born between 1965 and 1979 (Generation X) and 15% of those born between 1946 and 1964 (baby boomers).

India's management style norms may present a particular problem for millennial workers.

64%
of all Indian workers are forecasted to be millennials by 2021.

AND

13%
of millennial Indian workers are engaged at work.

Apathy among young workers is not strictly an Indian issue. All over the world, older managers and younger employees struggle to find common ground. However, the paternalistic system in India is built on the idea that experience and age bring wisdom. There's no room for the productive exchange of ideas when the "head of the family" is necessarily right and the young are necessarily unknowing. While breaking from tradition is never an effortless task, managers, especially of millennials, need to focus on individualized development, ongoing feedback and communication.

Reorienting Management Practices Will Help Indian Companies Ride the Wave of Change

All engagement initiatives start at the top. To improve engagement, leadership has to communicate that the company's operating behavior must change, why it must change, and how the company and workers will benefit from the change. But implementation of changes must take place at the level of individual workgroups and employees.

That's because engagement can't be commanded — it's cultivated. Engagement is an interpersonal and organic system in which everyone plays a part. But it starts at the top: Leaders create the conditions that engage, managers maintain the processes, and workers provide the energy and momentum that keep engagement alive. Fortunately, the mechanism to cascade engagement through Indian companies is entrenched — if leadership wants an engaged workforce, it has the authority to implement the conditions that engage. There will be resistance because change always provokes resistance. But India's already low engagement rates and the rise of the millennials certainly indicate that the time is ripe for a better workplace culture.

India doesn't have a moment to lose. Demonetization and digitalization are game-changers, and businesses that get it wrong will be left behind. The incentive to effectively handle engagement, performance management systems, individualized development and the management of a radically diversified workforce is enormous.

Of course, that's true for every company in every country. But in India, more so.

Leaders create the conditions that engage, managers maintain the processes, and workers provide the energy and momentum that keep engagement alive.

13

Australia/
New Zealand

Australia, New Zealand

14%

of employees in
Australia/New Zealand
are engaged.

% Employed full time
for an employer

44%   54%
Australia   New Zealand

See the appendix for "good jobs" data, by country.

71%

of employees in Australia/New Zealand are not engaged.

VS.

67%

globally

EMPLOYEES IN AUSTRALIA/NEW ZEALAND RATE their overall life higher than employees do in any other global region. On a scale from zero to 10, with zero being the "worst possible life" for them and 10 being the "best possible life," the average rating among employees in Australia/New Zealand is 7.36. The only other region in which employees' average life rating tops seven is the U.S./Canada, at 7.14.

Australia/New Zealand is one of two regions with relatively high employee life evaluations but relatively low workplace engagement scores.

Despite their employees' high overall life evaluations, employers in Australia/New Zealand face an ongoing conundrum. Gallup finds that workers in the region have lackluster employee engagement scores: Just 14% are engaged in their job, showing up every day with enthusiasm and the motivation to be highly productive. Another 15% of employees are actively disengaged — not only unhappy at work, but determined to undermine their colleagues' positive efforts. The remaining 71% of employees fall into the "not engaged" category; they show up each day but do just what is absolutely necessary to get through the day — and no more. Thus, Australia/New Zealand is one of two regions with relatively high employee life evaluations but relatively low workplace engagement scores (the other is Western Europe).

Gallup finds that workers in the region have lackluster employee engagement scores.

14%	71%	15%
engaged	not engaged	actively disengaged

AUSTRALIA/NEW ZEALAND AND WESTERN EUROPE HAVE HIGH LIFE EVALUATIONS BUT LOW ENGAGEMENT AT WORK

Average life evaluations vs. percentage engaged among employees

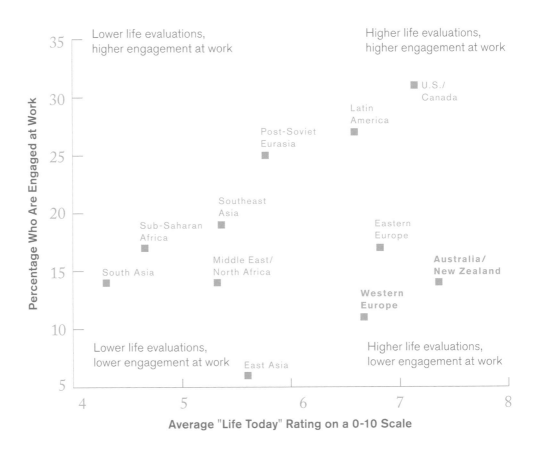

How can employers harness the overall satisfaction and enjoyment that Australians and New Zealanders have for their lives outside the office and bring that zeal into the workplace to boost productivity and economic gain? Four ways:

1. Give employees more opportunities to do what they do best.

2. Recognize that not everyone will make a good manager.

3. Create an employee proposition that emphasizes healthy work-life balance.

4. Maintain a workplace culture that engages and retains talented employees.

GIVE EMPLOYEES MORE OPPORTUNITIES TO DO WHAT THEY DO BEST

Australia and New Zealand are major players in the burgeoning Southeast Asian economy. Having recovered quickly from the 2009 global recession, both nations enjoy low unemployment and focus heavily on technology and innovation. But the potential for even greater success exists. Gallup's workplace research has long demonstrated that businesses with more engaged workforces have better business outcomes, including increased productivity and profitability. To grow their businesses in already-mature markets, leaders in the region must consider why their employees' enthusiasm for life is not fully reflected in how they feel about their job.

Just 21% of employees in Australia/New Zealand strongly agree with the statement "I like what I do each day" — a troublesome sign of their lack of emotional investment in their daily work life. Culturally, Australians and New Zealanders are known for their "can-do" spirit; therefore, strategies for improving outcomes through engagement need to resonate with people known for their rugged individualism. In that light, it is clear that employers need processes that identify employees' individual strengths and organizational flexibility that moves employees into roles that make use of those strengths.

RECOGNIZE THAT NOT EVERYONE WILL MAKE A GOOD MANAGER

Employees in Australia and New Zealand are often pragmatic, capable people who may not appear to need — or even want — much individualized attention from managers. Nevertheless, even the most self-reliant workers benefit from the support of a manager who thinks about how best to align each employee's personal goals and expectations with those of the organization they work for. Unfortunately, many business leaders in both countries continue to rely on hierarchy and technical skills when making managerial hiring decisions rather than explicitly identifying the managerial talent needed to maintain high levels of engagement among their workforces.

The best managers understand — and talk about — their natural talent for managing people, creating an atmosphere where employees are comfortable discussing their own strengths and weaknesses. Talented managers behave as coaches, meeting with individual employees on a regular basis to discuss ways they can more effectively use their unique strengths to contribute to the growth of the organization.

CREATE AN EMPLOYEE PROPOSITION THAT EMPHASIZES HEALTHY WORK-LIFE BALANCE

Work-life balance has various meanings that often include tactical and philosophical components for employees. Increasingly, people want to be able to adjust their hours and schedules as needed and to work remotely when they can without compromising work quality or productivity. That is why it's critical for employees to know how an organization "walks the talk" on greater work-life balance and well-being.

Organizations should highlight what they offer to help employees balance work and life and improve their well-being, but they also need to make this discussion about culture. Flextime and similar perks are attractive, but they are beneficial only when employees truly feel empowered to use them.

MAINTAIN A WORKPLACE CULTURE THAT ENGAGES AND RETAINS TALENTED EMPLOYEES

Retaining talented workers can be a challenge for employers in Australia and New Zealand where many, especially those in the millennial generation, are thinking about their next job opportunity. But engaged employees are less likely to have one foot out the door because time spent at work feels less psychologically burdensome, making it easier to maintain a healthy work-life balance.

Another look at their overall life evaluations demonstrates the result that engagement at work can have on the way employees view their life in general: Among engaged employees, the average life evaluation rating rises to almost eight (7.89) on the 0-10 scale, while among workers who are actively disengaged, it falls to well below seven (6.61).

When employees in Australia and New Zealand have enthusiasm for their work that matches their positive feelings about their life overall, they will have a sense of well-being that is among the highest in the world.

Even the most self-reliant workers benefit from the support of a manager who thinks about how best to align each employee's personal goals and expectations with those of the organization they work for.

14

Latin America

Argentina, Belize, Bolivia, Brazil, Chile, Colombia, Costa Rica, Dominican Republic, Ecuador, El Salvador, Guatemala, Haiti, Honduras, Jamaica, Mexico, Nicaragua, Panama, Paraguay, Peru, Puerto Rico, Uruguay, Venezuela

27%

of employees in Latin America are engaged.

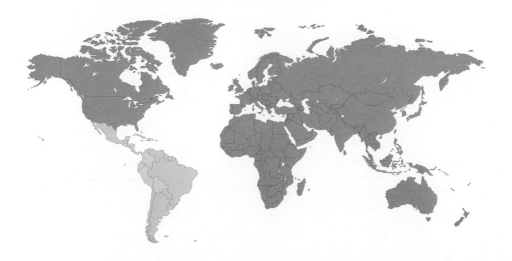

% Employed full time
for an employer

6%   41%
Haiti   Uruguay

See the appendix for "good jobs" data, by country.

32%

of working-age adults in Latin America say they are employed full time for an employer.

vs.

32%

globally

IN LATIN AMERICA, MANY COUNTRIES have struggled to rally since the end of the commodity boom in the 2000s. Those years of high growth raised expectations among many residents, who became accustomed to higher living standards. But the decline in commodity prices left those expectations largely unmet, resulting in increased social instability and political change. Good jobs are now relatively scarce in much of the region; Gallup finds that 32% of Latin American residents aged 23 to 65 say they are employed full time for an employer. By comparison, 56% of U.S./Canada residents in that age range say the same.

As in other regions around the world, many countries in Latin America have been experiencing "growing pains." Economic and social development strains and stretches societies as new ideas collide with tradition. Some countries in the region have struggled to adopt technological advances from abroad because of a lack of expertise, infrastructure and funds. In the political realm, populist movements highlight the ongoing — in some cases, widening — gap between wealthy elites and the vast majority who, in most countries, struggle to get by.

Some countries in the region have struggled to adopt technological advances from abroad because of a lack of expertise, infrastructure and funds.

Governments in the region have been criticized for not investing enough in infrastructure for human capital development during the boom years to improve social mobility. Access to high-quality education remains spotty, and in most countries, only well-connected elites are able to send their children to college. Education is critical for attracting investors and developing businesses. Just 15% of Latin Americans with eight years or less of formal education, versus 47% of those who have completed four years of education beyond high school, say they work full time for an employer.

In spite of a cultural bias toward positivity about their living conditions, Latin Americans are among the least likely to say they are satisfied with one other critical support for human capital development: healthcare. Just 42% of residents in the region tell Gallup they are satisfied with the availability of quality healthcare in their city or area, making Latin America one of the three regions — along with post-Soviet Eurasia (40% satisfied) and sub-Saharan Africa (43% satisfied) — with the lowest levels of healthcare satisfaction in the world. Much of the region is now experiencing increased prevalence of chronic conditions like cardiovascular disease, diabetes and cancer; these conditions substantially lower the potential for human capital-based development, particularly in communities with inadequate healthcare services.

WORKERS WHO PERFORM MANUAL LABOR ARE LEAST LIKELY TO BE THRIVING

The challenges associated with income inequality are clearly reflected in the daily experiences of Latin American workers, which vary substantially by occupation. Perhaps the most notable differences are between manual laborers and knowledge workers. Gallup asks residents to evaluate their current lives on a 0-10 scale and to predict where on the scale their lives will be in five years. The results classify them as "thriving," "struggling" or "suffering." (See the appendix for an explanation of the thriving, struggling and suffering categories.)

Just 37% of construction and manufacturing workers in the region fall into the thriving category, versus 66% of professional workers. Occupational type is related to workers' daily emotional state as well; for example, 22% of service workers and 20% of construction and manufacturing workers say they experienced sadness for much of the previous day, compared with 11% of professional workers.

These findings speak to the effect of status perceptions in Latin American societies — the gap between the haves and have-nots. Workplaces of all types need to ensure that employees feel respected and honored for their individual contributions.

EMPLOYEES' WELL-BEING INDICATORS VARY BY JOB TYPE IN
LATIN AMERICA

	Give "thriving" life ratings %	Experienced enjoyment much of the day yesterday %	Experienced sadness much of the day yesterday %
Professional: doctor, lawyer, engineer, teacher, nurse, etc.	66	90	11
Manager/Executive/Official: in a business or the government	59	88	15
Clerical/Other office worker/ Sales worker	52	83	17
Service worker: maid, taxi driver, maintenance or repair worker, etc.	49	79	22
Vendor/Small-scale trader/Self-employed/ Informal worker	46	85	19
Construction/Manufacturing/ Production worker	37	76	20

MANAGEMENT STRATEGIES SHOULD EMPHASIZE DEVELOPMENT OPPORTUNITIES AND PERSONAL RELATIONSHIPS

In many cases, outdated management practices may exacerbate class-based social divisions in Latin America. Cultural norms that emphasize respect for authority figures reinforce hierarchical structures in many facets of society — including workplaces. The authoritarian, top-down mentality has a firm hold on how organizations are structured and how they treat their employees.

Thus, many businesses in the region — particularly those in the large informal sectors of the region's economies — give employees' needs short shrift. Workers are often devalued by the perception that they can be easily replaced if they aren't productive or don't follow the rules. Further, employers fear that empowering workers might cause them to demand more or unionize. This mindset adds up to a general mistrust among all parties as the goals and needs of employees do not align with those of the organization they work for.

The region's employers can help offset the problems associated with inequality through management strategies that promote growth and development. Employers who provide workers with regular training opportunities will continually upgrade the quality of their workforce, offering individual firms a significant competitive advantage in the short term. Local governments should partner with such firms to ensure that any increased demand for adult education programs is met. Over time, development-focused management practices have the potential to reduce social tensions and inure the region's economies against volatile commodity cycles by establishing a more sustainable, human capital-based foundation for growth.

The good news is that in some Latin American countries, the prevalence of vertical management structures is beginning to wane as more organizations — including multinational businesses operating in the region — recognize the need to ensure all employees are engaged in their daily work life. Younger workers, in particular, are challenging traditional workplace hierarchies, seeking more egalitarian environments that offer developmental opportunities and freedom to express ideas. Companies know they are facing competition for talent and growth, and they are more aware of the need to pay attention to employee-centered metrics like engagement.

THE CHANGE TO EMPLOYEE-CENTERED MANAGEMENT IS AN INVESTMENT IN THE FUTURE

For many organizations, the transition from a hierarchical, low-trust organization to a more cohesive, horizontal structure requires a fundamental change in the role and mindset of managers. It will require careful selection of managers who understand the need for such a change, who respect each employee and who understand the synergy that results from aligning individual goals with those of the organization.

Gallup's workplace research indicates that the long-term gains in workforce productivity, safety and retention far exceed the short-term costs. Such changes have the potential to improve employees' sense of personal well-being — and to enhance the positivity they extend in their families and communities.

Employers who provide workers with regular training opportunities will continually upgrade the quality of their workforce, offering individual firms a significant competitive advantage in the short term.

15

United States/ Canada

United States, Canada

31%

of employees in the U.S./Canada are engaged.

% Employed full time
for an employer

56%
United States

58%
Canada

See the appendix for "good jobs" data, by country.

82%

*of engaged employees in the U.S./
Canada strongly agree that they
like what they do each day.*

vs.

71%

globally

IN THE U.S./CANADA, EMPLOYEES ARE more likely to be engaged than in any other region. However, with 31% engaged, ample room for improvement remains. Comparatively, the U.S./Canada region is among the most economically developed in the world, with a high proportion of professional and knowledge-based jobs, which tend to have somewhat higher engagement levels than do other employment categories. And unlike the collectivism in much of East Asia, a culture of individualism bolsters employee engagement in this region by maximizing the strengths and contributions of each employee.

Beyond relating to business metrics like productivity and retention, engagement in the U.S./Canada relates powerfully to the day-to-day experiences of these countries' employees: 82% of engaged employees in the combined population strongly agree that they like what they do each day, versus 42% of those who are not engaged and 19% of those who are actively disengaged at work. Similarly, 65% of engaged employees strongly agree that they learned or did something interesting the previous day, versus 30% of not engaged employees and 16% of those who are actively disengaged.

MOST ENGAGED EMPLOYEES IN U.S./CANADA LIKE WHAT THEY DO
% U.S./Canada employees who strongly agree with the statement "I like what I do each day"

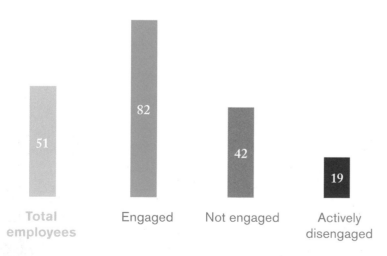

| Total employees | Engaged | Not engaged | Actively disengaged |
| 51 | 82 | 42 | 19 |

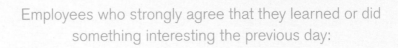

Employees who strongly agree that they learned or did something interesting the previous day:

65%
engaged

30%
not engaged

16%
actively disengaged

There is a significant difference in employee engagement levels among employed residents in each country, with Canada lagging the U.S. at 20% vs. 33%, respectively, based on data collected from 2014 to 2016. American employees are somewhat more likely than employed Canadians to strongly agree with several items gauging the 12 elements of engagement, particularly "I know what is expected of me at work" and "There is someone at work who encourages my development."

Female employees are somewhat more likely than male employees in Canada to strongly agree with these two items, helping lift overall engagement levels higher among employed women in the country than employed men (24% vs. 16%, respectively). This suggests a particular need to focus on expectations and development in job types that skew toward men in Canada, including construction and manufacturing.

Gallup's *State of the American Workplace* report contains in-depth analysis of current data on U.S. employees, including their engagement levels and changing expectations, as well as cutting-edge strategies for performance management. The report can be downloaded at Gallup.com.

U.S./CANADA SPOTLIGHT: THE U.S./CANADA PRODUCTIVITY GAP

Strengths-based workplaces could give Canadian firms a productivity boost.

Perhaps no country in the world invites comparison to the United States more than its neighbor to the north. Canada is another highly developed democracy with a diverse, well-educated workforce. It's understandable, then, when Canadian leaders fret that the country has for decades lagged behind the U.S. in labor productivity growth, a key economic indicator. Moreover, the gap has been widening in favor of the U.S. in recent years.

Analysts have offered various explanations for Canada's lower productivity growth. In recent years, the federal government has implemented an agenda targeting claims that the country lacks a sufficient culture of innovation. In *The Global Competitiveness Report 2016-2017*, the World Economic Forum (WEF) ranks Canada 15th in the world on its Global Competitiveness Index, while it ranks the U.S. third. Among the factors most likely to be seen as problematic for Canada in the WEF's Executive Opinion Survey is "insufficient capacity to innovate." Others have argued that improvements to Canada's infrastructure are needed to help close the productivity gap with the U.S.

Gallup's global workplace studies highlight another factor that may contribute to Americans' productivity advantage: Employees hold a stronger belief that they are working in a job that makes use of their innate abilities. In 2016, American employees were more likely than those in any other Organisation for Economic Co-operation and Development (OECD) country — including Canada — to strongly agree that at work, they have the opportunity to do what they do best every day.

This suggests that American workplaces are more adept than those in many other developed nations when it comes to providing employees with opportunities to apply the best of their natural selves — their strengths — in addition to their skills and knowledge. This fundamental aspect of engagement is among the most important to employees who are considering whether to take a job with a different organization, and it is one of the main reasons they choose to leave their job. When organizations and managers focus on giving people an opportunity to do what they do best, they can better attract, engage and retain employees.

American workplaces are more adept than those in many other developed nations when it comes to providing employees with opportunities to apply the best of their natural selves.

Canadian managers and business leaders may, thus, be able to enhance productivity in their teams by making more concerted efforts to match the right person with the right job. The best managers do this by:

- building a performance development environment where there is ongoing dialogue, awareness and recognition of strengths

- talking to each employee about the unique value that he or she provides to the team and organization

- making regular adjustments to align work, when possible, with team members' strengths

Ultimately, successful managers know the areas in which their employees excel and are able to position them accordingly so that they remain highly engaged while making the most of their innate talents.

In the U.S./Canada, employees are more likely to be engaged than in any other region. However, with 31% engaged, ample room for improvement remains.

Appendix 1

APPENDIX 1: METHODOLOGY NOTES

Most of the data in this report come from the Gallup World Poll, for which Gallup conducts nationally representative surveys annually in more than 150 countries around the world. Unless otherwise indicated, the findings presented here are based on data aggregated from three years of polling (2014, 2015 and 2016) in each country. The resulting sample sizes allow for more detailed analysis of employed residents and other subgroups within societies.

The Gallup World Poll

The Gallup World Poll continually surveys residents in more than 150 countries, representing more than 99% of the world's adult population, using randomly selected, nationally representative samples. Gallup typically surveys 1,000 individuals in each country, using a standard set of core questions that has been translated into the major languages of the respective country. In some regions, supplemental questions are asked in addition to core questions.

Telephone surveys are used in countries where telephone coverage represents at least 80% of the population or is the customary survey methodology. In Central and Eastern Europe, as well as in the developing world, including much of Latin America, the former Soviet Union countries, nearly all of Asia, the Middle East, and Africa, an area frame design is used for face-to-face interviewing. Face-to-face interviews are approximately one hour long, while telephone interviews are about 30 minutes long. In many countries, the survey is conducted once per year, and fieldwork is generally completed in two to four weeks.

Gallup is entirely responsible for the management, design and control of the Gallup World Poll. For the past 80 years, Gallup has been committed to the principle that accurately collecting and disseminating the opinions and aspirations of people around the globe is vital to understanding our world. Gallup provides information in an objective, reliable and scientifically grounded manner. Gallup is not associated with any political orientation, party or advocacy group and does not accept partisan entities as clients. Any individual, institution or governmental agency may access the Gallup World Poll regardless of nationality. The identities of clients and all surveyed respondents will remain confidential.

Life Evaluation Index

The Life Evaluation Index included among the standard set of core questions on the Gallup World Poll measures respondents' perceptions of where they stand now and in the future. Building on the Cantril Self-Anchoring Striving Scale,[1] Gallup measures life satisfaction by asking respondents to place the status of their lives on a "ladder" scale with steps numbered from zero to 10, where zero indicates the worst possible life and 10 the best possible life. Individuals who rate their current lives a "7" or higher AND their future an "8" or higher are "thriving." Individuals are "suffering" if they report their current AND future lives as a "4" and lower. All other individuals are "struggling."

- Please imagine a ladder, with steps numbered from zero at the bottom to 10 at the top. The top of the ladder represents the best possible life for you and the bottom of the ladder represents the worst possible life for you. On which step of the ladder would you say you personally feel you stand at this time?

- Please imagine a ladder, with steps numbered from zero at the bottom to 10 at the top. The top of the ladder represents the best possible life for you and the bottom of the ladder represents the worst possible life for you. Just your best guess, on which step do you think you will stand in the future, say about five years from now?

---

1   Cantril, H. (1965). *The pattern of human concerns*. New Brunswick, NJ: Rutgers University Press.

The final country-level index is a variable that codes respondents into one of three categories of well-being and represents the percentage of respondents in each category. Country-level weights are applied to this calculation.

Gallup's Q12 Client Database

In some cases, this report refers to discoveries based on Gallup's historical client database, which contains information from clients whose employees took the Q12 survey between 1996 and 2015. It includes data from 31 million respondents from 3.7 million workgroups and 2,161 clients in 198 countries and 14 major industries.

Gallup updates its database annually. Findings used to conduct research and set benchmarks are based on three-year rolling periods. Gallup's 2016 Q12 Client Database includes data from 2013, 2014 and 2015, with data from 6.5 million respondents, 821,000 workgroups and 279 clients in 159 countries and 14 major industries.

Appendix 2

APPENDIX 2: SUPPORT INFORMATION

Coaching Conversations Road Map: From *Re-Engineering Performance Management* Research Paper

Five Conversations That Drive Performance

Gallup's coaching conversations framework provides managers with a practical framework for how and when to execute the fundamentals of effective performance-oriented coaching conversations: establish expectations, continually coach and create accountability. The framework helps managers understand the key types of coaching conversations they should be having, how to approach the conversations and how to plan for them.

Through Gallup's five coaching conversations framework, managers learn the importance of spending disproportionately more time establishing expectations with their team by getting to know them, discussing why performance expectations exist and creating an open dialogue about the work they will be pursuing together. Only with a thorough understanding of current expectations can follow-up coaching conversations about how to achieve those expectations be effective.

Coaching conversations drive performance as coaches develop communication, managerial and people skills. A rapport between the manager and employee is initially formed through a role and relationship orientation conversation. As managers get to know team members as individuals and better understand each person's contributions to the team's success, they can more authentically connect with each person, understand team members' needs and individualize performance conversations. Then managers can more easily make coaching an everyday part of their routine by anticipating how to handle different types of coaching scenarios and planning the logistics of fitting all of the necessary coaching conversations onto their calendar.

Managers must also learn that "continually coach" doesn't mean simply that they should talk to their team more often. Rather, ongoing coaching conversations include a combination of informal quick connects, formal check-in meetings about workload and priorities, and developmental coaching opportunities that arise as work is being performed. It is critical that both managers and team members understand and appreciate the purpose of these conversations and when to have them.

For instance, a quick connect is the most powerful driver of employee engagement and must occur at least weekly. Without these touchpoints, engagement is likely to suffer. The most engaging coaches in the world have daily quick connects and do so through various communication modes, from hallway conversations to emails to phone calls to instant messages. By contrast, check-in meetings must be scheduled in congruence with the needs of the individual. Some people need frequent guidance, and others feel micromanaged when a manager asks for status updates often. Developmental coaching is a true art and arguably the most difficult type of conversation to master.

Finally, effective coaching must create accountability. As such, managers must schedule time to review performance progress and recalibrate expectations as performance needs change. Formal progress reviews should occur at least every six months and reflect the dialogue created during the other key types of coaching conversations that occur daily, weekly and monthly in between progress reviews. Progress reviews are a great coaching tool when they are focused on celebrating success, preparing for future achievements, and planning for development and growth opportunities.

By mastering these five key types of coaching conversations, managers can focus more of their time and efforts on the coaching moments that matter most.

Empowering People to Succeed With the CliftonStrengths Assessment

As of mid-2017, almost 17 million people around the globe had taken the CliftonStrengths assessment across 22 different languages.

English	French	Romanian
13,587,682	84,220	7,114
Chinese	Thai	Hungarian
514,099	73,243	4,634
Japanese	Polish	Indonesian
458,428	35,646	2,881
Spanish	Hebrew	Bulgarian
253,210	33,830	1,373
Korean	Italian	Turkish
213,409	22,300	1,334
German	Swedish	Croatian
195,194	17,589	1,240
Portuguese	Russian	
119,101	16,659	
Dutch	Arabic	
104,773	7,561	

EMPLOYEE ENGAGEMENT

Adults aged 23-65, Gallup World Poll, 2014-2016

	Engaged %	Not engaged %	Actively disengaged %
Afghanistan	17[5]	65[6]	18[5]
Albania	22[5]	64[6]	13[4]
Argentina	24[4]	62[4]	14[3]
Armenia	25[5]	65[6]	10[3]
Australia	14[3]	71[3]	16[3]
Austria	12[2]	71[3]	18[2]
Azerbaijan	7[2]	70[4]	23[4]
Bahrain	16[2]	67[3]	16[2]
Bangladesh	31[7]	57[7]	12[5]
Belarus	15[3]	59[4]	26[3]
Belgium	10[2]	73[3]	17[3]
Benin	12[4]	66[6]	22[5]
Bhutan	3[3]	92[4]	4[3]
Bolivia	28[5]	61[5]	12[3]
Bosnia and Herzegovina	13[4]	69[5]	18[4]
Botswana	16[4]	58[5]	26[5]
Brazil	29[5]	58[5]	13[3]
Bulgaria	18[3]	67[4]	15[3]
Burkina Faso	8[3]	66[6]	26[5]
Cambodia	21[5]	66[6]	13[4]
Cameroon	12[4]	70[6]	18[5]
Canada	20[3]	66[3]	14[2]
Chad	12[4]	64[6]	24[5]
Chile	30[4]	56[4]	13[3]
China	6[1]	75[2]	19[2]
Colombia	36[5]	54[5]	10[3]

Superscripted numbers represent the plus/minus percentage-point margin of sampling error for each figure. Margin-of-error estimates incorporate the influence of data weighting and are calculated at the 95% level of confidence.

	Engaged %	Not engaged %	Actively disengaged %
Congo (Kinshasa)	10[3]	70[5]	19[4]
Congo (Brazzaville)	27[6]	54[6]	20[5]
Costa Rica	32[4]	56[5]	12[3]
Croatia	13[3]	71[4]	15[3]
Cyprus	16[3]	65[3]	19[3]
Czech Republic	14[3]	65[4]	20[3]
Denmark	16[2]	73[3]	11[2]
Dominican Republic	33[5]	52[5]	15[4]
Ecuador	30[5]	61[5]	8[3]
Egypt	12[3]	65[5]	24[4]
El Salvador	34[5]	54[5]	12[4]
Estonia	20[3]	65[4]	15[3]
Ethiopia	8[4]	66[7]	26[6]
Finland	12[2]	76[3]	12[3]
France	6[2]	69[3]	25[3]
Gabon	14[3]	61[5]	25[4]
Georgia	26[5]	57[6]	17[4]
Germany	15[2]	70[2]	15[2]
Ghana	19[5]	68[6]	12[4]
Greece	11[3]	71[5]	17[4]
Guatemala	30[5]	59[6]	11[4]
Guinea	28[6]	60[7]	12[4]
Honduras	32[6]	53[6]	15[4]
Hong Kong	5[2]	67[4]	28[4]
Hungary	10[3]	66[4]	24[4]
Iceland	16[4]	76[5]	8[3]
India	13[2]	65[3]	22[2]

Superscripted numbers represent the plus/minus percentage-point margin of sampling error for each figure. Margin-of-error estimates incorporate the influence of data weighting and are calculated at the 95% level of confidence.

	Engaged %	Not engaged %	Actively disengaged %
Indonesia	15[4]	76[5]	10[3]
Iran	9[3]	67[5]	24[5]
Iraq	14[3]	64[4]	22[4]
Ireland	13[2]	71[3]	16[2]
Israel	16[3]	67[3]	18[3]
Italy	5[2]	64[4]	30[3]
Ivory Coast	15[4]	65[5]	20[5]
Japan	6[2]	71[3]	23[3]
Jordan	17[4]	63[5]	20[4]
Kazakhstan	29[4]	62[4]	10[2]
Kenya	18[4]	63[5]	19[4]
Kosovo	18[4]	65[5]	17[4]
Kuwait	15[3]	65[3]	20[3]
Kyrgyzstan	32[5]	51[6]	17[4]
Latvia	14[3]	71[3]	15[3]
Lebanon	17[3]	66[4]	18[3]
Liberia	32[7]	54[8]	14[5]
Libya	19[4]	64[5]	18[4]
Lithuania	11[2]	67[4]	22[3]
Luxembourg	8[2]	80[3]	13[2]
Macedonia	20[4]	61[5]	19[4]
Madagascar	18[5]	68[6]	13[4]
Malawi	16[5]	57[7]	28[6]
Malaysia	17[3]	70[4]	13[3]
Mali	20[6]	67[7]	13[5]
Malta	16[3]	70[3]	14[2]
Mauritania	24[5]	61[5]	15[4]

Superscripted numbers represent the plus/minus percentage-point margin of sampling error for each figure. Margin-of-error estimates incorporate the influence of data weighting and are calculated at the 95% level of confidence.

	Engaged %	Not engaged %	Actively disengaged %
Mauritius	18[4]	70[5]	12[4]
Mexico	23[4]	60[4]	17[3]
Moldova	15[3]	66[4]	19[3]
Mongolia	34[5]	57[5]	9[3]
Montenegro	18[3]	67[4]	15[3]
Morocco	20[5]	55[6]	25[6]
Myanmar	18[5]	62[6]	20[5]
Nepal	20[6]	60[8]	21[6]
Netherlands	12[2]	75[3]	13[2]
New Zealand	19[3]	71[3]	10[2]
Nicaragua	14[4]	75[5]	12[4]
Niger	12[4]	65[6]	23[6]
Nigeria	17[4]	73[5]	10[3]
Northern Cyprus	11[3]	66[5]	22[4]
Norway	17[2]	75[3]	8[2]
Pakistan	5[2]	73[5]	22[4]
Palestinian Territories	15[4]	63[6]	22[5]
Panama	39[4]	51[4]	10[3]
Paraguay	12[3]	63[5]	25[4]
Peru	22[4]	67[5]	12[3]
Philippines	36[5]	55[5]	9[3]
Poland	14[3]	73[4]	13[3]
Portugal	16[2]	70[3]	14[2]
Qatar	13[4]	69[6]	18[5]
Romania	22[4]	61[5]	17[4]
Russia	27[2]	60[3]	12[2]
Rwanda	17[4]	62[5]	21[4]

Superscripted numbers represent the plus/minus percentage-point margin of sampling error for each figure. Margin-of-error estimates incorporate the influence of data weighting and are calculated at the 95% level of confidence.

	Engaged %	Not engaged %	Actively disengaged %
Saudi Arabia	17[4]	62[5]	21[4]
Senegal	25[5]	65[5]	10[3]
Serbia	22[4]	60[4]	18[3]
Sierra Leone	37[7]	47[7]	15[5]
Singapore	23[4]	69[4]	8[2]
Slovakia	15[3]	66[4]	18[3]
Slovenia	13[2]	71[3]	16[3]
Somalia	20[5]	64[6]	17[5]
South Africa	15[3]	68[4]	18[3]
South Korea	7[2]	67[4]	26[3]
South Sudan	18[5]	64[6]	18[5]
Spain	6[3]	79[6]	15[5]
Sri Lanka	38[7]	54[7]	8[4]
Sweden	14[2]	75[3]	11[2]
Switzerland	13[2]	76[3]	12[2]
Taiwan	7[2]	70[3]	23[3]
Tajikistan	13[4]	73[6]	14[4]
Tanzania	17[5]	64[7]	18[5]
Thailand	23[5]	73[6]	4[2]
Togo	20[5]	58[6]	22[5]
Tunisia	13[3]	66[5]	21[4]
Turkey	17[4]	64[5]	18[4]
Turkmenistan	22[3]	74[3]	5[2]
Uganda	12[3]	61[5]	27[5]
Ukraine	12[3]	67[4]	20[3]
United Arab Emirates	16[2]	69[2]	16[2]
United Kingdom	11[2]	68[3]	21[3]

Superscripted numbers represent the plus/minus percentage-point margin of sampling error for each figure. Margin-of-error estimates incorporate the influence of data weighting and are calculated at the 95% level of confidence.

	Engaged %	Not engaged %	Actively disengaged %
United States	33^0	51^0	16^0
Uruguay	30^4	50^5	20^4
Venezuela	25^4	64^5	11^3
Vietnam	9^3	68^6	23^5
Zambia	19^5	59^6	22^5
Zimbabwe	11^4	63^6	25^6

Superscripted numbers represent the plus/minus percentage-point margin of sampling error for each figure. Margin-of-error estimates incorporate the influence of data weighting and are calculated at the 95% level of confidence.

GOOD JOBS

Adults aged 23-65, Gallup World Poll, 2014-2016	Employed full time for an employer %
Afghanistan	11
Albania	19
Algeria	23
Angola	18
Argentina	36
Armenia	22
Australia	44
Austria	49
Azerbaijan	28
Bahrain	62
Bangladesh	11
Belarus	63
Belgium	45
Belize	26
Benin	10
Bhutan	13
Bolivia	28
Bosnia and Herzegovina	27
Botswana	17
Brazil	33
Bulgaria	58
Burkina Faso	9
Burundi	7
Cambodia	16
Cameroon	13
Canada	58
Central African Republic	7

	Employed full time for an employer %
Chad	10
Chile	41
China	32
Colombia	31
Congo (Kinshasa)	15
Congo (Brazzaville)	15
Costa Rica	32
Croatia	56
Cyprus	51
Czech Republic	57
Denmark	58
Dominican Republic	32
Ecuador	26
Egypt	28
El Salvador	22
Estonia	66
Ethiopia	8
Finland	53
France	46
Gabon	22
Georgia	20
Germany	46
Ghana	12
Greece	34
Guatemala	20
Guinea	9
Haiti	6
Honduras	17

	Employed full time for an employer %
Hong Kong	50
Hungary	56
Iceland	60
India	31
Indonesia	25
Iran	14
Iraq	17
Ireland	39
Israel	57
Italy	36
Ivory Coast	14
Jamaica	20
Japan	49
Jordan	27
Kazakhstan	43
Kenya	22
Kosovo	19
Kuwait	39
Kyrgyzstan	19
Latvia	63
Lebanon	35
Lesotho	15
Liberia	6
Libya	22
Lithuania	61
Luxembourg	40
Macedonia	38
Madagascar	11

	Employed full time for an employer %
Malawi	10
Malaysia	37
Mali	7
Malta	49
Mauritania	15
Mauritius	42
Mexico	34
Moldova	39
Mongolia	37
Montenegro	41
Morocco	19
Mozambique	9
Myanmar	17
Namibia	18
Nepal	11
Netherlands	45
New Zealand	54
Nicaragua	23
Niger	5
Nigeria	15
Northern Cyprus	19
Norway	62
Pakistan	25
Palestinian Territories	19
Panama	32
Paraguay	36
Peru	28
Philippines	26

	Employed full time for an employer %
Poland	52
Portugal	51
Puerto Rico	37
Qatar	68
Romania	45
Russia	61
Rwanda	15
Saudi Arabia	36
Senegal	12
Serbia	46
Sierra Leone	7
Singapore	60
Slovakia	59
Slovenia	51
Somalia	9
South Africa	27
South Korea	43
South Sudan	6
Spain	37
Sri Lanka	24
Sudan	17
Sweden	67
Switzerland	46
Syria	21
Taiwan	51
Tajikistan	17
Tanzania	11
Thailand	30

	Employed full time for an employer %
Togo	9
Tunisia	27
Turkey	25
Turkmenistan	46
Uganda	19
Ukraine	46
United Arab Emirates	72
United Kingdom	50
United States	56
Uruguay	41
Uzbekistan	28
Venezuela	35
Vietnam	20
Yemen	8
Zambia	13
Zimbabwe	13

References

Untapped Human Capital: The Next Great Global Resource

Crabtree, S. (2016). Global prosperity hinges on closing jobs-education gap. Gallup. Retrieved from http://www.gallup.com/opinion/gallup/188222/global-prosperity-hinges-closing-jobs-education-gap.aspx?g_source=Crabtree&g_medium=search&g_campaign=tiles

Nink, M. (2013). Where disengagement at work is worse than joblessness. Gallup. Retrieved from http://www.gallup.com/businessjournal/163700/gbj-disengagement-worse-engagement-marco-nink.aspx?g_source=bad+managers&g_medium=search&g_campaign=tiles

High-Performing Workplace Cultures Need Engaged Employees

Most of the data in this report come from the Gallup World Poll, for which Gallup conducts nationally representative surveys annually in more than 150 countries around the world. Unless otherwise indicated, the findings presented here are based on data aggregated from three years' worth of polling (2014, 2015 and 2016) in each country. The resulting sample sizes allow for more detailed analysis of employed residents and other subgroups within societies.

For more methodological details about the Gallup World Poll, see page 188.

Meta-Analysis

Gallup's most recent meta-analysis accumulated 339 research studies across 230 organizations in 49 industries and 73 countries. Within each study, Gallup researchers statistically calculated the business-/work-unit-level relationship between employee engagement and performance outcomes that the organizations supplied. In total, Gallup studied 82,248 business/work units that included 1,822,131 employees. Gallup examined nine outcomes: customer loyalty/engagement, profitability, productivity, turnover, employee safety incidents, shrinkage, absenteeism, patient safety incidents and quality (defects).

Individual studies often contain small sample sizes and idiosyncrasies that distort the interpretation of results. Meta-analysis is a statistical technique that is useful in combining results of studies with seemingly disparate findings, correcting for sampling, measurement error and other study artifacts to understand the true relationship with greater precision. Gallup applied Hunter-Schmidt meta-analysis methods to 339 research studies to estimate the true relationship between engagement and each performance measure and to test for generalizability. After conducting the meta-analysis, Gallup researchers conducted utility analysis to examine the practical meaning of the relationships.

Earnings Per Share

The study included 17 publicly traded organizations that won the Gallup Great Workplace Award at least once from 2012 to 2016 and that met the following inclusion criteria: Gallup surveyed the majority of the organization (versus partial organization or subsidiary), 2011 to 2015 earnings per share (EPS) data were available, Q^{12} data for a minimum of two years from 2011 to 2015 were available, and the organization had a high Q^{12} response rate (minimum 80%, mean 93%). Gallup compared the difference in EPS for this group to their industry equivalents (top competitors that were not Gallup clients).

Harter, J. (2016, May 31). Moneyball for business: Employee engagement meta-analysis. Retrieved from http://www.gallup.com/businessjournal/191501/moneyball-business-employee-engagement-meta-analysis.aspx

Incentive Federation, Inc. (2016). Incentive marketplace estimate research study. Retrieved from http://www.incentivefederation.org/wp-content/uploads/2016/07/Incentive-Marketplace-Estimate-Research-Study-2015-16-White-Paper.pdf

International Monetary Fund. (2014). 25 years of transition: Post-Communist Europe and the IMF. Retrieved from https://www.imf.org/external/pubs/ft/reo/2014/eur/eng/pdf/erei_sr_102414.pdf

Mann, A., & Harter, J. (2016, January 7). The worldwide employee engagement crisis. Retrieved from http://www.gallup.com/businessjournal/188033/worldwide-employee-engagement-crisis.aspx

O'Boyle, E., & Harter, J. (2016, April 13). 35 organizations lead the world in creating cultures of engagement. Retrieved from http://www.gallup.com/opinion/gallup/190604/organizations-lead-world-creating-cultures-engagement.aspx

Training. (2015). Industry report. Retrieved from http://pubs.royle.com/publication/index.php?i=278428&m=&l=&p=22&pre=&ver=html5#{"page":22,"issue_id":278428}

Strengths-Based Team Leadership

Clifton, J. (2013). Build your career around your strengths, not your weaknesses. Gallup. Retrieved from http://news.gallup.com/opinion/chairman/169277/build-career-around-strengths-not-weaknesses.aspx

Ilgen, D. R., Fisher, C. D., & Taylor, M. S. (1979). Consequences of individual feedback on behavior in organizations. *Journal of Applied Psychology, 64*(4), 349-371. Retrieved from http://dx.doi.org/10.1037/0021-9010.64.4.349

Tapping Entrepreneurial Energy for Job Growth

Azeng, T. F., & Yogo, T. U. (2015). Youth unemployment, education and political instability: Evidence from selected developing countries 1991-2009. Retrieved from http://www.gsdrc.org/document-library/youth-unemployment-education-and-political-instability-evidence-from-selected-developing-countries-1991-2009/

Friedman, G. (2013). Europe, unemployment and instability. *Stratfor*. Retrieved from https://www.stratfor.com/weekly/europe-unemployment-and-instability

McCarville, B. (2016). Young entrepreneurs: Will they fix Mexico's economy? Gallup. Retrieved from http://www.gallup.com/businessjournal/191189/young-entrepreneurs-fix-mexico-economy.aspx

Western Europe

Alderman, L. (2010). Europe's two-speed economy: North vs. south. *The New York Times*. Retrieved from https://economix.blogs.nytimes.com/2010/07/28/europes-two-speed-economy-north-vs-south/

Florida, R., King, K., & Mellander, C. (2015). *The Global Creativity Index 2015*. Martin Prosperity Institute. Retrieved from http://martinprosperity.org/content/insight-the-2015-global-creativity-index/

Organisation for Economic Co-operation and Development. GDP per hour worked. Retrieved from https://data.oecd.org/lprdty/gdp-per-hour-worked.htm

Organisation for Economic Co-operation and Development. Hours worked. Retrieved from https://data.oecd.org/emp/hours-worked.htm

Eastern Europe

Atoyan, R. V., Christiansen, L. E., Dizioli, A., Ebeke, C. H., Ilahi, N., Ilyina, A. … Zakharova, D. V. (2016). Emigration and its economic impact on Eastern Europe. International Monetary Fund. Retrieved from https://www.imf.org/en/Publications/Staff-Discussion-Notes/Issues/2016/12/31/Emigration-and-Its-Economic-Impact-on-Eastern-Europe-42896

Labaye, E., Sjatil, P. E., Bogdan, W., Novak, J., Mischke, J., Fruk, M., & Ionutiu, O. (2013). A new dawn: Reigniting growth in Central and Eastern Europe. McKinsey Global Institute. Retrieved from http://www.mckinsey.com/global-themes/europe/a-new-dawn-reigniting-growth-in-central-and-eastern-europe

Winthrop, R., & McGivney, E. (2015). Why wait 100 years? Bridging the gap in global education. The Brookings Institution. Retrieved from https://www.brookings.edu/wp-content/uploads/2015/06/global_20161128_100-year-gap.pdf

Middle East/North Africa

Bteddini, L., & Heidenhof, G. (2012). Governance and public sector employment in the Middle East and North Africa. The World Bank. Retrieved from http://blogs.worldbank.org/arabvoices/governance-and-public-sector-employment-middle-east-and-north-africa

The World Bank. (2015). The economic outlook for the Middle East and North Africa - October 2015. Retrieved from http://www.worldbank.org/en/region/mena/brief/economic-outlook-middle-east-and-north-africa-october-2015

The World Bank. (2016). Private sector is key driver for growth in the Middle East and North Africa. Retrieved from http://www.worldbank.org/en/news/press-release/2016/07/24/private-sector-is-key-driver-for-growth-in-the-middle-east-and-north-africa

United Arab Emirates: The Cabinet. (2017). Mohammed Bin Rashid: Happiness & positivity are lifestyle, government commitment and a spirit uniting UAE community. Retrieved from https://www.uaecabinet.ae/en/details/news/mohammed-bin-rashid-happiness-positivity-are-lifestyle-government-commitment-and-a-spirit-uniting-uae-community

United Nations Development Programme. (2016). Arab human development report 2016: Enabling youth to shape their own future key to progress on development and stability in Arab region. Retrieved from http://www.undp.org/content/undp/en/home/presscenter/pressreleases/2016/11/29/arab-human-development-report-2016-enabling-youth-to-shape-their-own-future-key-to-progress-on-development-and-stability-in-arab-region-.html

Sub-Saharan Africa

Busteed, B. (2015). World agrees on need for better education systems. Gallup. Retrieved from http://www.gallup.com/businessjournal/187532/world-agrees-need-better-education-systems.aspx?g_source=internship&g_medium=search&g_campaign=tiles

International Monetary Fund. (2017). Regional economic outlook: Restarting the growth engine. Retrieved from http://www.imf.org/en/Publications/REO/SSA/Issues/2017/05/03/sreo0517

Kruger, N. (2016). South Africa has a skills shortage. How do we fix it? World Economic Forum. Retrieved from https://www.weforum.org/agenda/2016/05/south-africa-skills-shortage-how-do-we-fix-it/

The World Bank. (2017). Global economic prospects: Sub-Saharan Africa. Retrieved from http://www.worldbank.org/en/region/afr/brief/global-economic-prospects-sub-saharan-africa

East Asia

Asplund, J., & Fleming, J. H. (2008). When engaged employees meet engaged customers. Gallup. Retrieved from http://www.gallup.com/businessjournal/104170/when-engaged-employees-meet-engaged-customers.aspx

De Cremer, D., & Shaw, J. (2016). What China's shift to a service economy means for its managers. *Harvard Business Review*. Retrieved from https://hbr.org/2016/07/what-chinas-shift-to-a-service-economy-means-for-its-managers

Flade, P., Asplund, J., & Elliot, G. (2015). Employees who use their strengths outperform those who don't. Gallup. Retrieved from http://www.gallup.com/businessjournal/186044/employees-strengths-outperform-don.aspx?g_source=&g_medium=search&g_campaign=tiles

Kikkawa, T. (2006). Kigyo Shudan: The formation and functions of enterprise groups. *Business History*. Retrieved from http://www.tandfonline.com/doi/abs/10.1080/00076799500000055

Lewis, L. (2016). Japanese still suffer 'death by overwork' as long hours persist. *Financial Times*. Retrieved from https://www.ft.com/content/0cd29210-8dd1-11e6-a72e-b428cb934b78

Mann, A., & Harter, J. (2016). The worldwide employee engagement crisis. Gallup. Retrieved from http://www.gallup.com/businessjournal/188033/worldwide-employee-engagement-crisis.aspx

Nelson, C. (2011). Understanding Chinese consumers. *China Business Review*. Retrieved from http://www.chinabusinessreview.com/understanding-chinese-consumers/

Paine, L. S. (2010). The globe: The China rules. *Harvard Business Review*. Retrieved from https://hbr.org/2010/06/the-globe-the-china-rules

Rafferty, K. (2015). Why Abe's 'womenomics' program isn't working. *The Japan Times*. Retrieved from http://www.japantimes.co.jp/opinion/2015/12/31/commentary/japan-commentary/abes-womenomics-program-isnt-working/#.WZGDjmeWynd

Robison, J. (2010). The business case for wellbeing. Gallup. Retrieved from http://www.gallup.com/businessjournal/139373/business-case-wellbeing. aspx

Southeast Asia

Randstad. (2016). Media release: Singapore employees go into the new year with a positive outlook. Retrieved from https://www.randstad.com.sg/workforce360/articles/media-release-singapore-employees-go-into-the-new-year-with-a-positive-outlook

SkillsFuture. About SkillsFuture. Retrieved from http://www.skillsfuture.sg/what-is-skillsfuture.html#about2

United Nations Educational, Scientific and Cultural Organization. (2014). Education systems in ASEAN+6 countries: A comparative analysis of selected educational issues. Retrieved from http://unesdoc.unesco.org/images/0022/002267/226757E.pdf

South Asia

BBC News. (2015). Women struggle in India's family firms. Retrieved from http://www.bbc.co.uk/news/av/business-34717766/women-struggle-in-india-s-family-firms

Radjou, N. (2008). How Indian corporate culture impedes innovation. *Harvard Business Review*. https://hbr.org/2008/06/how-indian-corporate-culture-i

The World Bank. (2014). *Global Financial Development Report 2014: Financial Inclusion*. Retrieved from http://siteresources.worldbank.org/EXTGLOBALFINREPORT/Resources/8816096-1361888425203/9062080-1364927957721/GFDR-2014_Complete_Report.pdf

The World Bank. (2015). South Asia extreme poverty falls, but challenges remain. Retrieved from http://www.worldbank.org/en/news/press-release/2015/10/15/south-asia-extreme-poverty-falls-but-challenges-remain

Australia/New Zealand

Pash, C. (2016). Millennials are thinking about job changes so much, recruiters have coined a new name for them. *Business Insider Australia.* Retrieved from https://www.businessinsider.com.au/australian-millennials-are-so-busy-job-hopping-that-recruiters-call-them-continuous-candidates-2016-8

Latin America

Breene, K. (2016). 5 things to know about Latin America's economy. World Economic Forum. Retrieved from https://www.weforum.org/agenda/2016/01/5-things-to-know-about-latin-america-s-economy/

Rigoni, B., & Asplund, J. (2016). Global study: ROI for strengths-based development. Gallup. Retrieved from http://www.gallup.com/businessjournal/195725/global-study-roi-strengths-based-development.aspx?g_source=ROI&g_medium=search&g_campaign=tiles

Rojas-Suarez, L. (Ed.). (2009). Growing pains in Latin America: An economic growth framework as applied to Brazil, Colombia, Costa Rica, Mexico, and Peru. Retrieved from https://ssrn.com/abstract=2560941

Sabino, C. (2014). The true causes for Latin America's social inequality. *Pan Am Post.* Retrieved from https://panampost.com/carlos-sabino/2014/01/21/true-causes-latin-americas-inequality/

Sanguinetti, P. (2016). Skilling up: Human capital and Latin America. World Economic Forum. Retrieved from https://www.weforum.org/agenda/2016/12/skilling-up-human-capital-and-latin-america

United States/Canada

Hodgson, G. (2013). Canadian productivity: Even worse than previously thought. *The Globe and Mail*. Retrieved from https://beta.theglobeandmail.com/report-on-business/economy/economy-lab/canadian-productivity-even-worse-than-previously-thought/article13988435/?ref=http://www.theglobeandmail.com&

Schwab, K. (Ed.). (2016). The Global Competitiveness Report 2016-2017. World Economic Forum. Retrieved from https://www.weforum.org/reports/the-global-competitiveness-report-2016-2017-1

Shufelt, T. (2012). Canada's productivity gap is looking worse than ever. *Financial Post*. Retrieved from http://business.financialpost.com/executive/canadas-productivity-gap-is-looking-worse-than-ever